Ionian Islands

*A guide to genealogical sources in Corfu
and the other Ionian Islands,
including a transcript of graves from
British cemeteries in the Ionian Islands*

Justin Corfield

Corfield & Company
2000

Published by:
Corfield & Company
in conjunction with Gentext
37 Miriam St,
Rosanna 3084
Australia

© Copyright 2000
All Rights Reserved

Typeset by
Justin Corfield

Corfield, Justin J.
Ionian Islands:
A guide to genealogical sources in Corfu
and the other Ionian Islands,
including a transcript of graves from
British cemeteries in the Ionian Islands

Bibliography.
Includes Index
ISBN 1 876586 19 2

1. Ionian Islands (Greece) - Genealogy. I. Title.

929.3094955

Contents

General Historical Note	5
Bibliography of genealogical sources on the Ionian Islands 1815-64	7
Place Names	29
British Cemeteries in the Ionian Islands	31
Corfu	
Old British Cemetery	17
Small British Cemetery	105
Sant Rocco of New British Cemetery	116
Paxos	
Protestant Cemetery	158
Roman Catholic Cemetery	159
Santa Maura (Levkas)	
Protestant Cemetery	160
Roman Catholic Cemetery	164
Ithaca	
English Cemetery	166
Cephalonia	
British Cemetery	173
Zante	
English Cemetery	179
Protestant Cemetery	194
Catholic Cemetery	198
General Cemetery	202
Cerigo	
English Cemetery	205
Index	221
Index to Cemetery Inscriptions	223

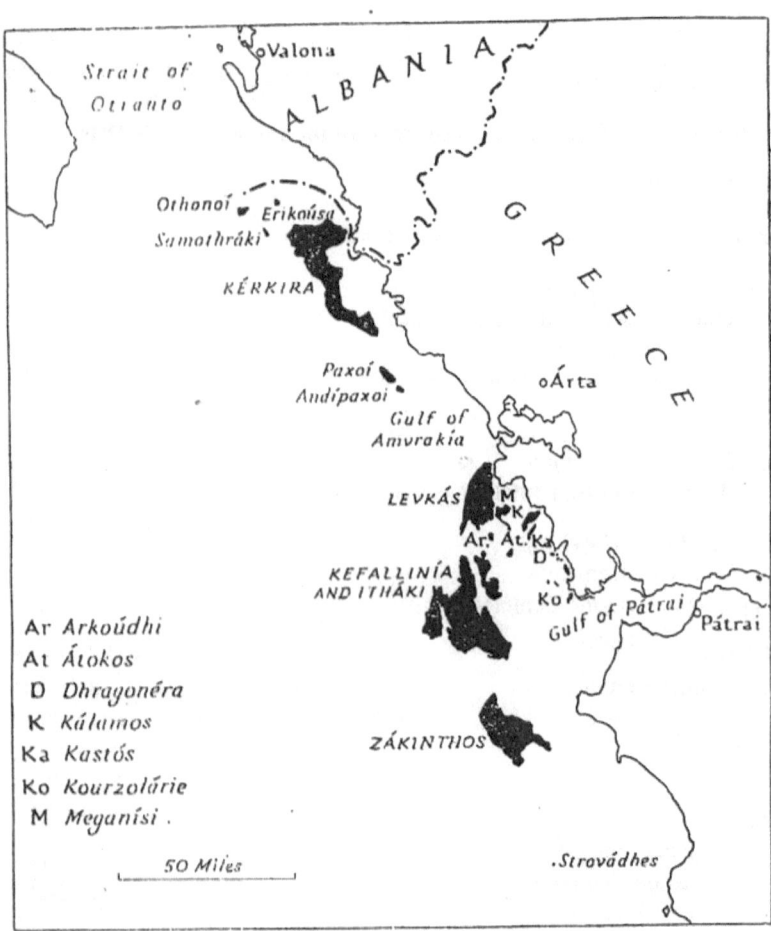

General Historical Note

The Ionian islands consist of seven islands off the coast of Albania and the Morea, and separated from the foot of Italy by the Ionian Sea. The largest of the islands is Corfu, and the others are: Paxos, Levkas, Ithaca, Cephalonia (Kefallinia), Zante (Zakinthos) and Cerigo (Kithira). The islands were occupied by the British from 1815-64. The islands were originally colonised by Corinth c700 BC, and were occupied by the Romans 229 BC. Although briefly occupied by Sicily (1147-54), they were semi-independent until 1386 when Venice annexed them, holding them, in spite of Turkish attacks in 1536 and 1716-18, until they were ceded to Napoleonic France in 1797. The islands had had contact with Britain since the sixteenth century when currants from Corinth and Zante made their appearance in English plum puddings.

In 1797 the Treaty of Camp Formio ended Venetian rule, and the French brought with them revolutionary ideas which the Corfiots (people from Corfu) took to readily. However French rule was short-lived and the Russians and Turks, allied together, seized the islands in 1799, and in the following year granted them nominal independence as the Septinsular Republic. However after the Peace of Tilsit in 1807, the Russians returned the island of Corfu to the French, amidst some local rejoicing. Their joy was tempered as efficient French taxation alienated the population and the Zantiotes and Cephalonians appealed to Britain for help. The French, offering concessions, restored the powers to the Senate of Corfu, in an attempt to placate the nobility.

As a part of the settlement at the end of the Napoleonic Wars, the Ionian Islands were placed under British protection in 1815. General Oswald took the surrender of the French garrisons and announced that the British were 'allies' and would establish a 'free and independent government' with full religious, civil and commercial rights. The flag of the Septinsular Republic was then flown alongside the Union Flag.

In 1811 the British started to establish a Government for the islands and in April 1812 local commerce was declared to be protected by the British. By 1814 trade with Britain amounted to less that £50,000 making annexation probably too costly. There were few major political developments until the outbreak of the Greek War for Independence in 1821. The Ionian Islands were keen to support the Greeks in the battle against the Turks, but were also eager to remain under British protection until the fighting had finished – during the 1830s there were 3,000 British soldiers posted to the Ionian Islands. As a result of this, and some judicious governing of the islands, they remained peaceful and in 1863, to support Britain's candidate for the Greek throne, the islands were offered as a form of dowry. Thus on 28 May 1864 they were returned to Greece. Since then many Britons have lived on the

Ionian islands – and it remains a popular tourist resort. As a result it has retained some British characteristics, and also is own version of cricket.

BRITISH GOVERNORS
1812-1815	James Campbell
1815-1824	Sir Thomas Maitland
1824-1832	Sir Frederick Adam
1832-1835	George Nugent Grenville, Lord Nugent
1835-1841	Howard Douglas
1841-1843	James Alexander Stewart Mackenzie
1843-1849	John Colborne, Lord Seaton
1849-1855	Sir Henry George Ward
1855-1859	John Young
1859	William Ewart Gladstone
1859-1864	Sir Henry Knight Storks

The population of the Ionian Islands during the British rule was estimated at from 200-240,000. Socially, the population is divided into several classes. The Venetians ruled through the old nobility, and these were the governing class at the time of the British Protectorate. These were generally Roman Catholic. The second class, that of merchants, had close connections with Britain; and the third class, of peasants, were Greek Orthodox, and spoke Greek. As can be seen from the cemetery inscriptions, most of the graves are of British soldiers and members of the British administration.

Bibliography of Genealogical Sources on the Ionian Islands 1815-64

Genealogical sources on the Ionian Islands during the period of British rule from 1815 until 1864 divide into five categories. The major sources are the records of the British administration (including the government gazette which notes governmental appointments etc), including registers of civil registration. These are held at the Public Record Office, London. There are also a number of histories of British rule (and of the island) and memoirs. Many recent books on Corfu and the other islands are produced for the tourist industry – some of these do, however, contain interesting accounts of British rule. The third category is that of unpublished papers of various Britons who lived on, or were connected with the Ionian Islands. The fourth category includes locally published books (and no doubt large numbers of locally-held papers). The last category is that of the physical evidence of the island – the buildings, the monuments and the cemeteries.[1]

For genealogists, it is worth noting that some of the sources (such as unpublished university theses) are only available at certain repositories, whereas some books and journal articles can be found in many major libraries around the world. The sources have been divided thematically, with some notes on them appended. For books and articles, the number of pages is noted to indicate the size and depth of coverage of the work. For simplicity in the case of books, preliminary pages etc have not been listed.

General Works on Corfu
Aspioti, Marie. *The Enchanted Isle of Corfu*, Corfu 1964, 1972, 1977.
Concina, Ennio & Nikiforou-Testone, Aliki. *Corfu: history, urban space and architecture 14th – 19th century*, Corfu 1994, pp. 182.
Dicks, Brian. *Corfu*, Newton Abbot 1977, pp. 190.
Foss, Arthur. *The Ionian Islands: Zakynthos to Corfu*, London 1969, pp. 272.
Jervis-White-Jervis, Henry. *History of the Island of Corfu...*, London 1852; Amsterdam 1970, pp. 323, genealogical chart.
Katsaros, Spiros. *A brief history of Corfu*, Kerkyra 1984, pp. 114.
Matton, Raymond. *Corfou*, Athens 1960, pp. 251. [In French.]
Stamatopoulos, Nondas. *Old Corfu: History and Culture*, Corfu 1978, pp. 296; Corfu 1993, pp. 325.

General Works on British Rule
Ansted, David Thomas. *The Ionian Islands in 1863*, London 1863, pp. 480.
Bowen, Sir George Ferguson. 'Ionian administration', *Quarterly Review* Vol 91 (Sept 1852), p315-52.

---

[1] I have not included biographies and autobiographies of Britons who have lived on Corfu in more recent times, eg Gerald Durrell.

Calligus, Eleni. 'Lord Seaton's reforms in the Ionian Islands 1843-8: a race with time', *European History Quarterly* Vol 24 (1994), p7-29.
Chircop, J. The British imperial network in the Mediterranean 1800-1870, PhD Thesis, Essex University 1997.
Coupland, Sir Reginald. *Britain in the Western Mediterranean*, London 1953, p160-67.
d'Istria, Dora. 'Les iles Ioniennes sous la domination de Venice et sous le protectorat britannique' [The Ionian islands under the rule of Venice and the British Protectorate], *Revue des deux Mondes* Vol 16 (15 July 1858), p408-11.
Dixon, Cyril Williams. *The Colonial Administrations of Sir Thomas Maitland*, London 1939, pp. 274; London 1968, pp. 274; New York 1969, pp. 274. [Although a history of the administration, it does contain a general history of British rule.]
Eldridge, C C. 'The myth of mid-Victorian 'separatism': the cession of the Bay Islands and the Ionian Islands in the early 1860s', *Victorian Studies* Vol 12 (1969), p331-46.
Gunning, Lucia Patrizio. The British Consular Service in the Aegean 1820-1860, PhD Thesis, University College, London 1997, pp. 307.
Hannell, David. 'A case of bad publicity: Britain and the Ionian Islands, 1848-51', *European History Quarterly* Vol 17 (1987), p131-43.
Hannell, David. 'The Ionian Islands under the British Protectorate: social and economic problems', *Journal of Modern Greek Studies* Vol 7/1 (1989), p105-32.
Hannell, David. 'Lord Palmerston and the 'Don Pacifco affair' of 1850: their connection', *European History Quarterly* Vol 19 (1989), p495-508.
Kinloch, A. *Santa Maura: a few pages upon that Island*, Edinburgh 1852.
Knox, Bruce. 'British Policy and the Ionian Islands, 1847-1864: nationalism and imperial administration', *English Historical Review* Vol 99, No 392 (1984), p503-29.
Orkney, George 6th Earl. *Four Years in the Ionian Islands*, London 1864, 2 Vols. [The memoirs of Viscount Kirkwall, as he then was, and an account of British rule.]
Pratt, Michael. *Britain's Greek Empire: Reflections on the History of the Ionian Islands from the Fall of Byzantium*, Totowa, NJ, 1981, pp. 206.
Seymour, Anthony. The Ionian Islands under the administration of George Granville, Lord Nugent, unpublished PhD Thesis.
Stavrinos, Miranda. 'The Reformist Party in the Ionian Islands (1848-1852): internal conflicts and nationalist aspirations', *Balkan Studies* [Greece] Vol 26/2 (1985), p351-61.
Tsitsonis, S E. 'An unpublished report (1858) by W E Gladstone on the political situation and administrative system in the seven islands (1815-1858)', *Balkan Studies* Vol 21/2 (1980), p287-329.
Tumelty, J J. The Ionian Islands under British Administration, PhD Thesis, Cambridge University 1952.
Wrigley, W David. 'Dissension in the Ionian Islands: Colonel Charles Napier and the Commissioners 1819-1833', *Balkan Studies* Vol 6/2 (1975), p12-22.
Wrigley, W David. *The Diplomatic Significance of Ionian Neutrality, 1821-31*, DPhil Thesis, Oxford University 1983; New York 1988, pp. 335.

Guidebooks
Bowman, John S et al. *Greek Islands*, New York 1999, pp. 404. [Frommer's Guide series. The Ionian islands: p344-64.]
Dubin, Marc. *The Greek Islands*, London 1997, pp. 400. [Eyewitness Travel Guide series. The Ionian Islands: p64-87.]

Gill, John. *Corfu & the Ionian Islands*, London 1997, pp. 272. [The Rough Guide series.]
Willett, David. *Greece: a lonely planet travel survival kit*, Hawthorn, Vic 1998, pp. 747. [Lonely Planet series. Ionian islands: p669-703.]
Young, Martin. *The Traveller's Guide to Corfu and other Ionian Islands*, London 1981, pp. 327.

Memoirs & Biographical Works

Bobou-Stamate, V. 'Anekdota Grammatika Tou Lordou Guilford (1827) se heirografo tes Gennadeiou Vivliothekes (mss 108): prote parousiase' [Unpublished letters by Lord Guilford (1827) in a manuscript from the Gennadion Library (MSS 108): first presentation], *Ellenika* [Greece] Vol 41/1 (1990), p59-77.
Bowen, Sir George Ferguson. *The Ionian Islands under British Protection*, London 1851, pp. 142.
Bowen, Sir George Ferguson. *Ithaca in 1850*, London 1851, pp. 68.
Bowen, Sir George Ferguson. *Thirty years of Colonial Government*, London 1889, 2 Vols.
Cochran, Peter. ''Nature's gentler errors': Byron, the Ionian Islands and Ali Pacha', *The Byron Journal* No 23 (1995), p22-35.
Dandolo, Antonio. *Des iles Ioniennes sous le protection Britannique* [The Ionian isles under British protection], Corfu 1851.
Davy, J. *Notes and observations on the Ionian Islands and Malta*, London 1842, 2 Vols.
Dixon, Cyril Williams. *The Colonial Administrations of Sir Thomas Maitland*, London 1939, pp. 274; London 1968, pp. 274; New York 1969, pp. 274. [Although a history of the administration, it does contain a good general history of British rule.]
Durrell, Lawrence. *Lear's Corfu: an anthology*, Corfu 1965, pp. 38.
Giffard, E. *A short visit to the Ionian Islands, Athens & the Morea*, London 1837, pp. 399.
Gilchrist, Hugh. *Australians and Greeks. Volume 1: The Early Years*, Rushcutters Bay, NSW 1992, pp. 432. [Includes much on the Bowen family, and also some other colonial officials who later moved to Australia.]
Hills, Mrs N L. *Life of Sir Woodbine Parish*, London 1910, pp. 454. [Chapter 5 relates to the Ionian Islands.]
Lear, Edward. *The Corfu Years: a chronicle presented through his letters and journals*, edited and introduced by Philip Sherrard, Athens 1988, pp. 244.
Lear, Edward. *Views in the Seven Ionian Islands*, London 1864; Oldham, Lancs 1979, pp. 25.
Lord, Walter Frewen. *Sir Thomas Maitland, the masters of the Mediterranean*, New York 1897, pp. 301.
Müller, Christian. *Journey through Greece and the seven Ionian Islands*, London 1822, pp. 96.
Napier, Charles James. *Memoir on the Roads of Cephalonia*, London 1825; Athens 1977, pp. 106.
Vaudoncourt, F G de. *Memoirs of the Ionian Islands...*, London 1816, pp. 502.
Williams, H W. *Travels in Italy, Greece and the Ionian Islands*, Edinburgh 1820, 2 Vols.
Wrigley, W David. 'Fourteen secret British documents concerning Count John Capodistrias (February-March 1828)', *Südost-Forschungen* [West Germany] Vol 45 (1986), p89-121.

Biographical Dictionaries
The usual sources of British biography provide much information on many Britons who lived in the Ionian Islands: Burke's *Peerage & Baronetage*, Burke's *Landed Gentry*, *The Dictionary of National Biography* and Boase's *Modern English Biography*. *Who's Who*, published in its current form since 1897, is too late to cover many of the people, but Bowker Saur's *British Biographical Index* is a phenomenal source, although its price restricts it to only major public and university libraries. For non-Britons on the islands, there is a very important genealogical work which does contain much on Greek and Albanian families.

Sturdza, Mihail Dimitri. *Grandes Familles de Grèce, d'Albanie et de Constantinople* [Great Families of Greece, Albania and Constantinople], Paris 1983, pp. 657. [Large well-illustrated book of family histories, biographies, family trees etc. In French.]

Some Britons connected with Corfu

Herbert, Sir Arthur James (1820-1897). The second son of John Arthur Jones of Llanarth Court, Monmouthshire, he reverted to the old family name of Herbert by Royal Licence. Educated at Prior Park Catholic College and Munich University, he joined the Royal Welch Fusiliers in 1839 and served as a Major in the Crimean War. In 1857 he was deputy Quartermaster-General at Corfu. Returning to England, he joined the House Guards and was gazetted Brigadier-General in 1873, and three years later, as Major General, commanded Dublin and the Curragh districts. He died 24 Nov 1897. See *Who's Who*.

Hull, Commander Thomas A (-1904). A naval officer, he was employed in the search for Sir John Franklin 1848-54, and from 1860-66 was involved in surveys of Palestine, Corfu, Tunis and Sicily. For the next six years he worked on the compilation of the Admiralty Wind and Current Charts of the World. Superintendent of Admiralty Charts, he was Inspector of Admiralty Charts of the Mercantile Marine at his death on 25 March 1904. See *Who's Who*.

Bowen, Sir George Ferguson (1821-1899). See page 113.

Crummer, James Henry (1792-1867). Born in Ireland, the son of Samuel Crummer, he served in the British Army at Copenhagen and then in the Peninsular War. As an officer in the 28th Regiment, his unit was posted to the Ionian Islands during the Greek War of Independence and was commandant of Calamos 1821-28. Whilst there, in 1827, he married Katerina Georgia Plessos, niece of Lord Byron, and in 1829 returned to Ireland. Six years later the family moved to Sydney, New South Wales, Australia, and was a magistrate in the Newcastle area, just north of Sydney. See *Australian Dictionary of Biography* Vol 1.

Hall, James (1784-18--). The second surgeon working in the (British) Royal Navy in Corfu in 1807, he managed to get away from the Ionian Islands when the French captured the islands. Being appointed surgeon in the navy, he accompanied convicts to Australia in 1822, briefly serving there during which time he gained an unfavourable reputation. He was later posted to Bermuda. See *Australian Dictionary of Biography* Vol 1.

Le Mesurier, Col Cecil Brooke (1831-1913). An artillery officer, he served in the Second Afghan War 1878-80. In 1854 he married Countess Nicolina, eldest daughter of Count Spiridione Zancarol of Corfu. See *Who's Who*.

Lowry, Lieutenant-General Robert William (1824-1905). The son of Capt W Lowry, Royal Navy, of Drumeagh, Dungannon, he was educated at Gracehill, the Royal School of Dungannon and the Belfast Academy. Lowry was ADC to Lord High Commissioner, Corfu, and Resident of Zante, serving in the Crimean War in the 47th Regiment of Foot. He commanded the Field Force against the Fenian Raid at Fort Erie in 1866. He died 8 June 1905. See *Who's Who*.

Schaw, Major-General Henry (1829-1902). The son of J S Schaw, Royal Artillery, he was educated at the Woolwich Academy and was a Prizeman in Mathematics and Fortifications. Commissioned in the Royal Engineers in 1847, he served at Chatham, Ireland, Ceylon, Crimea, Woolwich and then back at Chatham before being posted to Corfu where his responsibility was to dismantle the British fortifications when the island was handed back to Greece in 1864. Professor at the Staff College, he retired and advised the governments of New South Wales, Victoria and New Zealand on defences. He died in New Zealand on 14 August 1902. See *Who's Who*.

Sinclair, Dr James (1832-1910). Born at Berwick-on-Tweed, the eldest son of James Sinclair and Margaret (née Atkinson), he attended Edinburgh University and gained a commission in the Army Medical Department from the Royal College of Surgeons, Edinburgh, in 1853. Serving in Ceylon until 1857, he was then with the 2nd Queen's Royal Regiment in Malta, Corfu, Santa Maura, Zante and then Gibraltar until 1863. He later served in Bombay and then in Abyssinia. From 1876 he was Principal Medical Officer at Bermuda, Belfast, South Africa, Aldershot, Ireland, Malta, Ireland again, and was forced into retirement on account of his age in 1892. He lived in Belfast until his death, 21 November 1910 in Belfast. See *Who's Who*; Peterkin, A & Johnston, William. *Commissioned Officers in the Medical Services of the British Army*, London 1968, Vol 1.

Stanmore, 1st Baron (Arthur Gordon Hamilton) (1829-1912). Born in London, the fourth son of the 4th Earl of Aberdeen, he was educated at Cambridge University (MA 1851) and was Private Secretary to the Prime Minister, Earl of Aberdeen (his father) 1852-55. Member of Parliament for Beverley from 1854-57, he was Secretary on the Special Mission to Corfu 1858-59. He then had numerous colonial postings: Lieutenant-Governor of new Brunswick 1861-66, Governor of Trinidad 1866-70, Mauritius 1871-71, Fiji 1875-80, New Zealand 1880-82, Consul-General, Southern Pacific 1877-82 and Governor of Ceylon 1883-90. He wrote many books including a biography of his father. Created 1st Baron Stanmore in 1893, he died 1 January 1912. See *Who's Who*; Burke's *Peerage and Baronetage*.

Willis, Sir George Henry Smith (1823-1900). Born in Hampshire, the oldest son of George B Willis, Royal Artillery, of Sopley Park, Hampshire, he joined the 77th Regiment of Foot and served at Malta and then at Corfu. He was later posted to Jamaica, Nova Scotia, and then served with distinction during the Crimean War and then in Africa. He died 29 November 1900. See *Who's Who*.

Wynyard, Edward Buckley (1788-1864). Born in London, the son of Lieutenant-General William Wynyard, he joined the British Army and in 1808 he served under Lieutenant-General Sir John Oswald in the Ionian Islands and was severely wounded on 22 March 1810 at Santa Maura. Recuperating in Malta, he later served at St Helena and then was posted to New South Wales, Australia where he was a member of the Executive Council 1848-53 and the Legislative Council 1848-51. Wynyard Square in Sydney is named after him. See *Australian Dictionary of Biography* Vol 2.

Archives & Libraries

The major source for papers on the Ionian Islands under British rule is the Public Record Office, London. They are held under the Colonial Office Papers; and also Foreign Office Papers; and they are described in more detail in Anne Thurston's book. She notes that when the Protectorate ended, the complete archives were moved to London (p54). As a result it is possible to search for details on most Britons (and many others) who were living on the Ionian islands during British rule.

Kolyv-Karaleka, Marianne. 'Les archives des Iles Ioniennes: bibliographie orientative' [The archives of the Ionian Islands: bibliography for orientation], *Rassegna degli Archivi di Stato* [Italy] Vol 46/1 (1986), p53-64. [This lists guides to and inventories of archives of Corfu and other Ionian islands, which are among the richest and best preserved in Greece.]

List of Colonial Office Records preserved at the Public Record Office, London 1911, pp. 377. [Ionian Islands: p152-67.]

Thurston, Anne. *Records of the Colonial Office, Dominions Office, Commonwealth Relations Office and Commonwealth Office*, London 1995, p265-66.

Public Record Office, London

CO 136   Ionian Islands: original correspondence etc, from 1802 to 1873, 1433 vols.
CO 350   Ionian Islands: register of correspondence from 1849 to 1910, 6 vols.

Extracts in:
CO 728   Honours: register of correspondence from 1859 to 1940, 21 vols.
CO 879   Confidential print: Africa, from 1848 to 1961, 190 vols.
CO 326   General registers, from 1623 to 1849, 358 vols.
CO 714   Index to correspondence, from 1795 to 1874, 171 vols.
CO 537   Colonies General: supplementary original correspondence, from 1759 to 1955, 7862 vols and files.

Other papers which include information on the Ionian Islands include those of Lord Seaton which are held at Beechwood, Sparkwell, Devon; and the Grey papers (of Earl Grey, Prime Minister 1832-33) held at the Department of Palaeography and Diplomatic, 5 The College, Durham.

Church Records

The Anglican Churches in the Ionian Islands hold the registers of baptisms, marriages and burials for Corfu, Zante etc. The extracts which follow were transcribed by John Hopwood and appeared in *The Manchester Genealogist* Vol 13/3 (July 1977), p79; and Vol 14/1 (Jan 1977), p12-14.

Avouris, Spyros. *Brève histoire de l'Eglise des iles Ioniennes* [Brief history of the Church in the Ionian Islands], Athens 1956.

Purcell, Mary (ed). 'Dublin Diocesan Archives: Murray Papers', *Archivium Hibernicum* [Ireland] No 37 (1982), p29-121. [Lists papers of Archbishop Daniel Murray 1831-44, including letters about Catholics in the Ionian Isles.]

Extracts from the Parish Register in Corfu

Baptisms

1865

Jan 18	Wise	Victoria, daughter of George Wise, brewer of Corfu, and Mary Sava. Born 6 Dec 1864.
March 1	Page	Alexandra Adelaide, daughter of Edward Thomas Page, chemist of Corfu, and Emma. Born 29 Nov 1864.
March 5	Quinland	Wilhelmina Elizabeth Henrietta, daughter of Charles Quinland, shopkeeper, and Eliza Flack. Born 8 July 1864.
Oct 1	Page	Alexander Wilhelm, son of Mathew John Page, tailor of Corfu, and Susannah Emily.

1866

Feb 1	Stretch	Sophia, daughter of John Stretch, ship's chandler of Corfu, and Rosine.
Feb 1	Quinland	Edith Alice, daughter of Charles Quinland, shopkeeper, and Eliza Flack. Born 11 Feb 1866.
Nov 11	Whitfield	Edith Maud, daughter of James Whitfield, curator, British Cemetery, Corfu, and Sarah.
Dec 29	Wise	George Spiridion, son of George Wise, brewer of Corfu, and Mary.

1867

Feb 24	Page	Henrietta Esther, daughter of Edward T Page, chemist, and Emma.
June 14	Yarnley	Annie, daughter of William Richard Yarnley, banker of Patras, and Lucy Jane.
June 24	de Norman	Grace Ellen, daughter of John de Norman, Superintendent of Telegraphs, Corfu, and Harriett. Born 31 Jan 1867.
Aug 29	Wilkin	Ida Jane Caroline, daughter of John Wilkin, livery stable keeper, Corfu, and Emily. Born 15 July 1867.
Aug 29	Stretch	John Henry, son of John Stretch, ship's chandler of Corfu, and Rosine. Born 29 March 1867.
Nov 3	Salter	Sidney Arthur, son of George Piggott Salter, Chaplain of Corfu, and Elizabeth. Born 25 Sept 1867.
Nov 17	Page	Francis Woodley, son of Matthew John Page, tailor of Corfu, and Susannah Emily. Born 11 Sept 1867.
Dec 1	Acco ?	Joseph Samuel, son of Jehudah Acco?, tailor of Corfu, and Speranza Ano. Born in 1845 of Jewish parents.

1868

Feb 12	Quinland	Marianne Helen, daughter of Charles Quinland, merchant of Corfu, and Eliza Flack. Born 11 Jan 1868.
Sept 18	Haselmere	John Hartley, son of Joseph Haselmere, merchant of Alexandria, Egypt, and Emma Maria. Born 25 Aug 1869.

1869

March 31	Wilkin	Marianne Helen, daughter of John Wilkin, livery stable keeper, Corfu, and Emily.
May 5	Page	Victor Louis, son of Matthew John Page, tailor, and Susannah Emily. Born 8 March 1869.
Sept 2	Page	Leopold Dorset, son of Edward Thomas Page, chemist of Corfu, and Emma. Born 10 July 1869.
Nov 15	Hancock	Katherine Irene, daughter of Edward Hancock, merchant of Patras, and Caroline. Born 3 July 1869 at Patras.

1870

April 10	West	Arthur Thomas, son of Frederick West, Lieut Colonel residing in Corfu, and Emily.
Sept 25	Wilkin	Anne Charlotte, daughter of John Wilkin, livery stable keeper, Corfu, and Emily.

1871

June 8	Frey	Johanna Magdalina, daughter of John Frey, merchant of Corfu, and Amelia.
June 18	Page	Ida Annie, daughter of Matthew John Page, tailor of Corfu, and Susannah Emily.

1872

Jan 1	Page	Walter Thomasson of Edward Thomas Page, chemist of Corfu, and Emma.

Marriages

1866

Aug 30 — John Wilkin, 30, livery stable keeper, son of Joseph Wilkin, tradesman; and Emily Coulling, 25, daughter of James Coulling, gardener.

1867

May 4 — Johannes Frey, 28, merchant's clerk, son of Ulright Frey, grocer and Amelia Doser, 31, daughter of Joseph Doser, surgeon.

1872

Oct 29 — Demetrius Macropoulos, servant in the Household of the King, son of George Macropoulos, officer in the Greek Army; and Emily Mariner, nurse in the Household of the King, daughter of James Mariner, land steward. After marriage in Greek Church.

1875

June 24 — William Bainbridge Fletcher, surgeon, Royal Navy, son of William Fletcher, Rector of N--, Dorset; and Christine Adrianne Sidney Hughes, minor, daughter of John W C Hughes, Consular Chaplain.

1876
Feb 10   Henry Painter Goodridge, chaplain, HM Mary, son of George Thomas Goodridge, gentleman; and Theodora, Countess Bulgari, daughter of Count Cristochilo Bulgari, nobleman.
Aug 10   William Charlton Bolton-Johnson, aged 25, Lieutenant in the Royal Navy, son of George Johnson; and Leila Louisa Condi, daughter of Demetrio Costa Condi.

1877
June 2   George Thomas Beal, widower, auctioneer, son of John Beal, employer; and Anne Forrest, daughter of Robert William Forrest, late Captain, Ionian Militia.

1878
June 1   Charles Quentin Gregan Crawford, Lieutenant, HMS *Rapid*, son of Robert G Crawford, late officer, HM Army, and Esmeralda Harriet Calligary, daughter of Nicole Calligary, gentleman.
Aug 24   Heinrich C Beckman, German, and Angolina Qualermani, also German.

1879
May 5   John William Barnett, carpenter, son of Melia Barnett, engineer; and E Caridi, daughter of Alexander Caridi, shoemaker.

1881
Dec 13   Charles George John Kluppel, son of Balthasagar Joseph Kluppel, merchant; and Frances Helen Whitfield, daughter of James Fraser Whitfield, civilian.

1883
Dec 3   Ernest Frederick Hartman, farmer, son of August Hartman, bank cashier; and Euridiki Artavanis, son of Constantin Artavanis, farmer.

1884
July 24   Arthur Hill, merchant, son of John Hill, merchant; and Evanthira Toole, daughter of Ernest Toole, German Consul at Cephalonia.

Burials

1865
April 6   George Nicholls, master of *Solena*, aged 34 years.
June 16   Robert Hines, Royal Marine, HMS *Gibraltar*, aged 21 years.
June 29 (sic) Wilhelmina Elizabeth Henrietta Quinland, aged 1 year.
June 27   Thomas Peat, aged 82 years.
Nov 4   Victoria Vise, aged 13 months.
Nov 15   Thomas Davies, HMS *Gibraltar*, aged 21 years.
Dec 30   Robert Reid, HMS *Terrible*, aged 20 years.

1866
Feb 27   James Woodhouse, aged 83 years.

1867
Jan 23 Kate Parker, aged 1 year.
March 12 Catherine Groves, aged 80 years.
April 20 The Hon Robert Le Poer Trench, Royal Navy, aged 57 years.

1869
Jan 25 Joanne Henriette Phillipine Guibert, aged 44 years.
March 11 William Weale, V C at Mep?, aged 60 years.
June 15 Magdalene Burns, aged 35 years.
Oct 11 Marianne Helen Wilkin, aged 10 months.

1870
July 6 Rev G P Sutton, aged 35 years.

1871
May 29 Anne Charlotte Wilkin, aged 11 months.
June 12 Dr McMahon, HMS *Prince Consort*, aged 33 years.
Nov 24 Ida Annie Page, aged 8 months.

1872
March 23 George Hogarth Rainy, of Roasy, NB [New Brunswick?], aged 27 years. Removed to UK 28 March 1872.
May 23 Mary Vachain (née Roberts), aged 28 years.
July 8 Ann Carter, aged 80 years.
Dec 31 William Ward, seaman, yacht *Gelert*, RSYC, aged 27 years.

1873
Sept 16 Gladys Carlisle Conway Hughes, aged 2½ years.

1874
Jan 25 Georgiana Mary Lady Sebright, aged 41 years.
Nov 5 William Goodrunn, seaman, aged 22 years.
Aug 22 Babette Hoffman, passenger, Austrian *Vesta* from Alexandria, aged 42 years.
Sept 9 Mercy Knocker, aged 76 years.
Sept 18 Gertrude Evelyn, aged 14 years.

1875
Aug 3 Richard Weale, ex-Vice Consul, aged 45 years.
Aug 12 Amelia Manetta (née Broughton), aged 60 years.
Oct 18 James Hatherley, seaman, HMS *Devastation*, aged 36 years.
Nov 27 Edward Cope, seaman, SS *Kedor*, aged 19 years.
Dec 9 Thomas Carling, Master Brig *Lady Rothsay*, aged 55 years.

1876
March 16 William Crozier, of Dublin, aged 58 years.

1878
July 10 William D'Everell, ex-Captain of Port, aged 62 years.
Aug 20 Matthew John Page, aged 58 years.

Civil Registration

A series of registers covering births, marriages and deaths in the Ionian Islands, 1818-64, are held at the Family Records Centre, 88 Rosebery Avenue, London EC1 (which has replaced St Catherine's House). They are also available on microfiche in many genealogical libraries around the world. Alas they certainly do not include every birth, marriage or death in the Ionian Islands – in fact their coverage is quite sparse. The first page of the index for the register of deaths is given below. Records of baptisms, marriages, deaths and burials in Zante are held at the Public Record Office (RG 33/82). In addition, records of Baptisms 1865-1974 and Marriages 1866-1946 are held at the Society of Genealogists, London.

Deaths in the Ionian Islands

Appleby, Thomas	Corfu	8/2
Aubrey, Anne Jane	vido	8/3
Aubrey, Charlotte	vido	8/2
Baker, Frances	Corfu	6/5
Bell, Eliza White	Corfu	8/4
Bowden, Robert James	Gibraltar	8/1
Bradshaw, Elizabeth Jane	Corfu	8/11
Bradshaw, Frederick William	Corfu	8/11
Breakwell, Alfred C	Corfu	8/15
Brewer, Harriet	vido	8/1
Brosman, Patrick	Cephalonia	8/6
Brosman, Patrick	Cephalonia	7/2
Broughton, Jane	Zante	8/5
Broughton, Thomas	Corfu	6/6
Browne, Laura	Cephalonia	7/1
Browne, Laura	Cephalonia	8/6
Carrett, Charles	Corfu	6/7
Cartwright, John William	Corfu	8/12
Cavanagh, William	Corfu	8/17
Clayton, Alfred Robert	Corfu	8/18
Clayton, Emily Robertina	Corfu	8/2
Clunan, Mary	Cephalonia	7/1
Clunan, Mary	Cephalonia	8/6
Conally, Michael	Corfu	8/11

Diplomatic Records

Arch, G L. L'influence de la Revolution Française dans les Balkans: d'après les documents des archives de politique exterieure de la Russie [The influence of the French Revolution in the Balkans: documents in Russian foreign policy archives], *Etudes Balkaniques* [Bulgaria] Vol 27/1 (1991), p34-39. [Describes Russian archives which are now open to the public.]

Heppner, Harald. 'Österreichische pléne zur herrschaft über die Ionischen Inseln [Austrian plans for governing the Ionian Islands], *Balkan Studies* Vol 26/1 (1985), p57-72.

Wrigley, W D. 'The British enforcement of Ionian neutrality against Greek and Turkish refugees, 1821-1828: a study in selectivity', *Südost-Forschungen* [West Germany] No 46 (1987), p95-112.

Wrigley, W D. 'The issue of Ionian neutrality in Anglo-Ottoman Relations, 1821-1830', *Südost-Forschungen* [West Germany] No 47 (1988), p109-43.

Jewish Communities

The synagogue in Corfu, dating from the seventeenth century, is open to the public on Saturdays (from 9am until the evening).

Kaufman, David. 'Contributions à l'histoire des juifs de Corfou' [Contributions to the history of the Jews of Corfu], *Revue des Etudes Juivres* Vol 32 (1896), p226-34; Vol 33 (1897), p64-76 & 219-32; Vol 34 (1897), p263-75.

Preschel, Pearl Liba. The Jews of Corfu, PhD Thesis, New York University 1984, pp. 173.

Medals

For records on the Order of St Michael and St George, created for Malta and the Ionian Islands, these are held at the Public Record Office, Kew. The book by Paul Lambros covers coins issued under Venetian rule from 1730-97, coins and medals of the republic of the Ionian Islands 1801-07 and coins and medals issued under the provisional occupation by Britain 1809-15.

Lambros, Paul. *Coins and medals of the Ionian Islands*, Amsterdam 1968, pp. 80.

Thurston, Anne. *Records of the Colonial Office, Dominions Office, Commonwealth Relations Office and Commonwealth Office*, London 1995, p267.

Military Records

British *Army Lists* are published annually but these only list officers. For records on non-commissioned officers and privates, records are detailed in the book by Michael and Christopher Watts. The book by Norman Holding may not seem, at first sight, relevant. However it does contain useful information on the location of regimental archives, addresses etc.

Barnes, John D. 'The 35th Foot in Walcheren and the Ionian Islands', *Sussex Family Historian* Vol 6/6 (June 1985), p217-19. [About Robert Barnes, born 1792, who was posted to Corfu.]

Butler, L. 'Minor expeditions of the British Army: XI-Capture of the Ionian Islands', *United Services Magazine* Vol 32 (1906), p295-302.

Gregory, Desmond. 'A defence policy for the Ionian Islands - some wrong conclusions drawn by soldiers and statesmen', *Journal of the Society for Army Historical Research* Vol 64, No 257 (1986), p24-33.

Holding, Norman & Swinnerton, Iain. *The Location of British Army Records 1914-1918*, Bury, Lancs 1999, pp. 120.

Pappas, Nicholas Charles. Greeks in Russian Military Service in the late eighteenth and early nineteenth centuries, PhD Thesis, Stanford University 1983, pp. 621. [Includes references to the Ionian Islands.]

Rodger, N A M. *Naval records for genealogists*, London 1988, pp. 220.

Watts, Michael J & Christopher T. *My ancestor was in the British Army*, London 1995, pp. 124.
Wildy, Ted. 'Naval Ancestors', *The Genealogist* (AIGS, Australia) Vol 7/4 (Dec 1992), p144-45.

The Greek War of Independence

Crawley, C W. *The question of Greek Independence*, Cambridge 1930, pp. 272.
Crawley, C W. *John Capodistria: some unpublished documents*, Thessaloniki 1970, pp. 109.
Dakin, Douglas. *British and American Philhellenes during the Greek War of Independence 1821-1833*, Thessaloniki 1955, pp. 246.
Dakin, Douglas. *British intelligence of events in Greece 1824-1827*, Athens 1959, pp. 184.
Dontas, Domna N. *The last phase of the War of Independence in Western Greece*, Thessaloniki 1966, pp. 187.
Gordon, Thomas. *History of the Greek Revolution*, London 1832, 2 Vols.
Kaldis, W P. *John Capodistrias and the modern Greek state*, Madison, Wis 1963, pp. 126.
Woodhouse, C M. *Capodistria*, Oxford 1973, pp. 544. [About John Capodistria.]

Police Records
Gallant, Thomas. 'Peasant ideology and excommunication for crime in a colonial context: the Ionian Islands (Greece), 1817-1864', *Journal of Social History* Vol 23/3 (1990), p485-512.

Postal Services
During the British rule over the Ionian Islands, only four stamps were issued. The first as a British stamp overprinted 'Paid at Corfu' and the other three were a set (½d, 1d, 2d). These were printed by Perkins, Bacon & Co, issued on 15 May 1859, and had the inscription: 'ΙΟΝΙΚΟΝ ΚΡΑΤΟΣ. As the stamps are much more valuable in used condition than in an unused state, forgers have stuck many unused ones only old envelopes and stamp dealers do (and researchers should also) treat such documents with caution.

School Records
The Ionian Academy was formally inaugurated on 29 May 1824, occupying the former palace of the Proveditore Generale in the Old Fortress. By the end of the first academic year it had enrolled 211 students. By 1827 it had a library of 21,000 books, many donated by Guildford and other benefactors. The British also established a secondary school on each island – there were a total of twelve secondary schools in 1823, 29 by 1827 and 60 by 1832 (with a total enrolment of 2,500).

Shipping Records
Wrigley, W D. The neutrality of Ionian Shipping and its enforcement during the Greek Revolution (1821-1831)', *Mariner's Mirror* Vol 73/3 (1987), p245-60.

The First World War

During the First World War Corfu was used as a rest camp for the Serbian army, with some British soldiers convalescing there. These were from the remnants of the Serbian army after its retreat over the Albanian Highlands. Twelve Britons were buried in the Corfu British Cemetery – their graves are maintained by the Commonwealth War Graves Commission (listed below). There are also the graves of Italian soldiers during the First World War in a nearby cemetery.

Brincat, Off Ck 2nd Class Carmelo. HMS *Berberis*. Died 16 Dec 1918, aged 44. Son of Joseph and Antonia Brincat. Husband of Clothilde Brincat of 3 Piazza Fosse, Floriana, Malta. Grave No 35.

Busson, Cpl Cyril. 9th Bn, Gloucestershire Regt. Died 23 June 1918. Grave No 22.

Ellison, Pte Cyril. Royal Army Medical Corps (Corfu Convalescent Hospital). Died. Died 2 Oct 1918, aged 27. Son of Edward and Mary Ellison of 15 Limekiln Lane, Poulton, Wallasey, Cheshire. Grave No 29.

Gulley, Stoker PO Lewis Joseph. HMS *Bacchus*. Died of dysentery, 31 July 1918, aged 30. Son of Nathaniel and Eliza Gulley of Plymton, Devon; husband of Alice M Gulley of 35 Greville Rd, Plymouth. Grave No 25.

Hoskin, Off Std Ernest William. HMS *Aquarius*. Died 6 Aug 1918, aged 27. Son of Frances Emily Clark (formerly Hoskin) and A H Clark (stepfather) of 18 Young St, Derby. Grave No 27.

Lewis, Lieut Charles Anthony. Royal Navy Volunteer Reserve. HMS *Egmont*. Died 17 Dec 1918, aged 24. Son of Charles and Maud Lewis of 4 South Rd, Devonshire Park, Birkenhead. Grave No 36.

Phillips, Cpl Horatio Lloyd. Base Details, Royal Field Artillery (formerly 98th Bde). Died 6th April 1918, aged 23. Son of E J and Joan Phillips of Rose Cottage, Gwaelodygarth, Taffs Well, Cardiff. Grave No 21.

Rogers, Stoker PO John Henry. HMS *Badger*. Died 23 Oct 1918, aged 31.

Routledge, Lance-Corporal Charles Allison. Military Foot Police, Military Police Corps. Died 6 July 1918, aged 26. Son of Robert and Mary G Routledge of Faceby, Stokesley, Yorks. Grave No 23.

Warner, Deck Hand Fred. Royal Navy Reserve, HMML *No 33*. Died 4 Aug 1918. Son of C and E C Warner of 99 Island Wall, Whitstable, Kent. Grave No 26.

Williamson, Pte W. 2nd Bn, East Yorkshire Regiment. Died of pneumonia, 10 Aug 1917, aged 25. Brother of Mrs E Stanbra of 19 Brook St, Brook Hill, Sheffield. Grave No 18.

Wood, Engineman George. HM Trawler *Strephon*. Died of pneumonia 12 Oct 1918, aged 23. Son of James and Elsie Wood of 20 King Edward St, Fraserburgh. Grave No 30.

The Second World War

The Ionian Islands were occupied by the Italians during the Balkan Campaign of April 1941, and when the Italian government signed the armistice in September 1943 the Germans overwhelmed them on Corfu,

Levkas and Zante. On Cephalonia the Germans took control but not after more than a thousand Italians were killed in combat – with others shot out of hand at the end of the fighting.

Giraudi, Giovanni. *A Cefalonia e Corfu si combatte: testimonianza di un superstite della leggendaria Divisione Acqui*, Milan 1982, pp. 217.

La Divisione Acqui a Cefalonia e Corfu: settembre 1943-novembre 1944, Bologna 1975, pp. 94.

Corfu Channel Dispute/Operation Retail

In October 1946 there was a naval dispute between Albania and the United Kingdom, known as the Corfu Channel Incident (or Operation Retail), in which forty British sailors died. It began with the cruisers *Superb* and *Orion* being fired on in May 1946 after they sailed through the Corfu Channel which Albania claimed as her territorial waters. On 22 Oct 1946 two Royal Navy destroyers, the *Saumarez* (Captain William H Selby) and the *Volage* (Commander R T Paul) were badly damaged when they hit mines in the Channel, with an officer and 37 ratings being killed instantly and two officers and 43 ratings being injured. Other destroyers involved in mine-sweeping in the area were the *Leander*, the *Ocean*, the HMS *Surprise*, the *Orion* and the *Matapan*. Of those killed, some ten bodies were recovered and these were buried at Corfu. The injured were taken to Malta, where a few more are believed to have died and been buried.

As a result the British Government seized gold belonging to the former Albanian Government (which was held by the Tripartite Commission for Restitution of Monetary Gold). As a result the UK and the Socialist Republic of Albania did not establish diplomatic relations until the gold issue was settled in Sept-Oct 1996. On 22 October 1996 there was a commemoration service held in the British cemetery at Corfu.

Curiously lists of the Foreign Office papers on the Corfu Channel incident have been excised from the Foreign Office catalogues published in the 1980s and 1990s.

'The Albanian Gold Mystery', *World War II Investigator* (Sept 1988), p2-7.

'Baron Phillips: Obituary', *The Daily Telegraph* (3 May 1997). [Baron (his Christian name) John Phillips was the mining expert for Operation Retail.]

Davie, Michael. 'Gun-boat diplomacy that lost lives - but won gold', *The Observer*, London) 21 April 1985, p46.

Dodds, Stan. *Albanian Incident*, London 1983, pp. 138. [Novel.]

Gardiner, Leslie. *The Eagle spreads his claws,* Edinburgh 1966, pp. 286. [The best general history.]

Leggett, Eric. *The Corfu Incident*, London 1974, pp. 183.

Vox Militaris (pseud). '50th Commemoration of the Corfu Incident', *Army & Defence Quarterly Journal* Vol 127/1 (1997), p91-92.

Wilson, William. 'Albania', *Contemporary Review* Vol 239 (Aug 1981), p71-75.

Wright, Quincy. 'The Corfu Channel Case', *American Journal of International Law* Vol 43 (July 1949), p491-94.

Each sailor was commemorated by a plain wooden cross bearing the date, the sailor's name and his ship. Their graves are maintained by the Commonwealth War Graves Commission.

Bevan, Stoker Leslie Oliver. RN. HMS *Saumarez*. Died 23 Oct 1946. Son of Thomas and Mary Bevan; husband of Dorothy Lydia Bevan of Newport. Plot 8. Grave No 11.

Briffa, Asst Steward Victor Emmanuel. RN. HMS *Saumarez*. Died 23 Oct 1946. Plot 8. Grave No 1.

Clark, Gnr George Alexander. Royal Artillery. Died 24 Jan 1945. Age 29. Son of George Alexander and Jane Elizabeth Clark; husband of Hilda Mary Clark of West Cross, Glamorgan. Plot 2. Grave No 14. [Not from Operation Retail.]

Crossley, Stoker Kenneth. RN. HMS *Barford*. Died 25 Jan 1945. Age 25. Son of George Henry and Sarah Ann Crossley of Levenshulme, Manchester. Plot 2. Grave No 13. [Not from Operation Retail.]

Denattista, Ldg Steward Antonio. RN. HMS *Saumarez*. Died 23 Oct 1946. Plot 8. Grave No 2.

Eva, Ldg Cook Stanley John. RN. HMS *Saumarez*. Died 23 Oct 1946. Age 28. Son of Frederick Eva and Ellen Eva of Plympton, Devon. Plot 8. Grave No 7.

Hales, AB Gordon Henry. RN. HMS *Saumarez*. Died 23 Oct 1946. Age 20. Son of Henry and Alice Hales of Bristol; husband of Patricia Hales of Knowle, Bristol. Plot 8. Grave No 5.

Keeton, Stoker Cyril. RN. HMS *Volage*. Died 23 Oct 1946. Age 39. Son of Frederick and Grace Keeton; husband of Ivy Keeton of Porchester, Hampshire. Plot 8. Grave No 10.

Knott, PO Joseph. RN. HMS *Volage*. Died 23 Oct 1946. Age 23. Son of Joseph Venning Noel Knott and of Dorothy Mary Knott (née Gates). Plot 8. Grave No 9.

Leonard, Marine Thomas. Royal Marines Commando. Died 9 Nov 1944. Age 26. Son of Elizabeth Leonard of Leeds, Yorkshire. Plot 8. Grave No 15. [Not from Operation Retail.]

McKenna, Cpl George. Royal Marines Commando. Mentioned in Despatches. Died 26 Oct 1944. Age 25. Son of George and Mary Ellen McKenna of Middleborough, Yorkshire. Plot 8. Grave No 16. [Not from Operation Retail.]

Morris, Cook Ronald. RN. HMS *Saumarez*. Died 23 Oct 1946. Plot 8. Grave No 3.

Sayers, Ldg Stoker William Harry. RN. HMS *Saumarez*. Died 23 Oct 1946. Age 25. Son of Ralph and Eva Sayers of Eccles, Lancashire; husband of Emily Sayers of Eccles. Plot 8. Grave No 8.

Weaver, Ldg Seaman John. RN. HMS *Saumarez*. Died 23 Oct 1946. Age 26. Son of Peter and Agnes N Weaver of Maryhill, Glasgow. Plot 8. Grave No 12.

Winter, Ldg Radio Mechanic Brian James. RN. HMS *Saumarez*. Died 23 Oct 1946. Age 18. Son of Arthur James Winter and Winifred Annie Winter of Poynings, Sussex. Plot 8. Grave No 6.

Winterbottom, AB Sam. RN. HMS *Saumarez*. Died 23 Oct 1946. Age 26. Son of Sam and Sarah Ann Winterbottom of Hyde, Cheshire. Plot 8. Grave No 5.

How to locate books or journal articles etc

There are many sources for genealogical research. Although the large genealogical libraries, such as that of the Society of Genealogists in London, may have a number of the titles listed in this work, most of the sources cited are not specifically aimed at a genealogical audience and it will be necessary to look for them in a library or bookshop.

Books

For books, some of the more common ones may be held at a local public library. However for many of the more specialized ones it may be essential to use a major public library or a university library. Most libraries have computerised catalogues and for books you can search for the book by the author or by the title. Most of the very university libraries have catalogues on the internet, and it is often possible to check the holding of a particular library before going there. To purchase copies of the relevant books, an high street bookshop would be able to locate any books in print, and a bookshop specialising in secondhand books may be able to locate those titles not currently in print. For many specialist titles, both in print and secondhand, because they may have been produced in short print-runs, they can be expensive to purchase.

Magazine/Journal Articles

For magazine/journal articles, you should search a library catalogue by the title of the magazine or journal. Most computerised catalogues will also give the span of their collection (eg last six months, since 1990 etc). Although many libraries keep back-copies of magazines such as *Time* magazine, the more obscure academic journals such as the *Journal of the Society for Army Historical Research* have a small circulation and would only be held in university libraries. If you are keen to purchase your own copy of a particular issue, many journal publishers do keep back-copies which they will sell to you, and specialist bookshops may also hold back-copies of journals.

Newspaper articles

Newspapers are extremely useful sources of information and many large public libraries and university libraries used to hold bound copies of the more important ones. However with the pressure on space and also the need for many university libraries to maintain complete sets of many newspapers, a large number of newspaper titles have been microfilmed and are held in the library in a special section devoted to microfilm. It is usually possible to print from microfilm.

University Theses

One of the most valuable sources of information for genealogists can be found in university theses. These range from BA (Honours) Theses, through MA (Master's) Theses to PhD/DPhil (Doctoral) Theses and vary in length from 10,000 to 150,000 words. When completing a thesis, the student submits three or four bound copies of the thesis. After the thesis is marked and deemed to have reached the required standard for the particular degree, one copy of the thesis is returned to the student, one retained by the University supervisor, and one held by the University departmental library. With a PhD Thesis, a further copy is usually deposited in the main University library. Some of the theses are later published, and although the published work may take into account later developments, corrections and the like, for a specialist topic it can be important to track down the original thesis as it may contain extra footnotes for sources, a more comprehensive bibliography etc. The footnotes are important as they may direct researchers to particular newspaper articles, archival repositories etc. However a thesis can often only be consulted in the University which the student was attending when it was completed. With Doctoral theses (and some Masters theses), the University of Michigan has published a number of these in bound black volumes (or on microfilm). Thus large academic libraries hold theses from all over the world. It is also important to note that sometimes an archives/library stipulates that if students use their resources for research, they must donate a copy of the completed thesis to that repository. This has meant that some national archives and research institutes have many theses which would otherwise be hard to find.

Inter-library Loans

The Inter-library loan system is one by which users of one library may seek books or articles from another library. This operates in some public libraries and all academic libraries. A fee is usually payable and there are usually three levels of charges: for a book which has been found in a library within one's own country; for a book which has to be brought in from overseas; and for an article (when usually only a photocopy will be supplied).

Place Names

This listing notes the major settlements and places in the Ionian Islands (by the present spelling of their names) and which island they are located on. In this book I have used the British spellings: Corfu, Paxos, Levkas (Santa Maura), Ithaca, Zante, Cefallonia and Cerigo rather than the current spellings: Corfu, Paxos, Lefkáda, Ithaki, Zakinthos (or Zakynthos), Kefallonia and Kythira.

Place Name	Location
Acharávi	Corfu
Afiónas	Corfu
Agalás	Zante
Agia Efthimía	Cefallonia
Agía Pelagia	Cerigo
Agía Sofia Cave	Cerigo
Agía Thekla	Cefallonia
Agios Dimítros	Cefallonia
Agios Geórgios	Cerigo
Agios Ioánnis	Ithaca
Agios Mattháios	Corfu
Agios Nikitas	Levkas
Agios Nikólaos	Zante
Agios Pétros	Levkas
Agios Spyrídon	Cefallonia
Agios Spyrídon	Cefallonia
Agrílion	Cefallonia
Alykés	Corfu
Angoí	Ithaca
Ano Korakiána	Corfu
Antipaxos	Small island south of Paxos
Argási	Zante
Argostoli	Cefallonia
Argyrádes	Corfu
Asos	Cefallonia
Astoupádes	Cefallonia
Avlaki	Corfu
Avlemonas	Cerigo
Benítses	Corfu
Chalkós	Cerigo
Chlomós	Corfu
Chora	Cerigo
Dasiá	Corfu
Diakófti	Cerigo
Dilináta	Cefallonia
Dragótina	Corfu
Drogkaráti Cave	Cefallonia
Eláti Stavróta	Levkas
Epískepi	Corfu

Place Name	Location
Episkópi	Corfu
Ermones	Corfu
Exogi	Ithaca
Fársa	Cefallonia
Filiatró	Ithaca
Fiskárdo	Cefallonia
Fónissa	Cerigo
Fragkáta	Cefallonia
Frátsia	Cerigo
Frikes	Ithaca
Friligkiánika	Cerigo
Fyrí Ammos	Cerigo
Gaios	Paxos
Geráki	Zante
Giannádes	Corfu
Glyfáda	Corfu
Gouviá	Corfu
Hora (see Chora)	Cerigo
Kaladía	Cerigo
Kalámi	Corfu
Kalamítsi	Levkas
Kálamos	Cerigo
Kalokairinés	Cerigo
Kampi	Zante
Kanópi	Corfu
Kapsáli	Cerigo
Karavás	Cerigo
Karosádes	Corfu
Kassiópi	Corfu
Kastri Point	Cerigo
Kástro	Cefallonia
Káto Chora	Cerigo
Kávos	Corfu
Kavvadádes	Corfu
Kióni	Ithaca
Komponáda	Cerigo
Korisíon Lagoon	Corfu
Koríthi	Zante
Kouloúra	Corfu
Laganás	Zante
Lagópodo	Zante
Lákka	Paxos
Lákones	Corfu
Lássi	Cefallonia
Lefkáda	Levkas
Léfki	Ithaca
Lefkímmi	Corfu

Place Name	Location
Limnária	Cerigo
Limniónas	Cerigo
Lipádes	Corfu
Livádi	Cerigo
Lixoúri	Cefallonia
Markópoulo	Cefallonia
Meganisi	Small island off the east coast of Levkas
Melidóni	Cerigo
Melissani Cave-Lake	Cefallonia
Mesongi	Corfu
Miniá	Cefallonia
Mitáta	Cerigo
Moní Agios Ioannis sto Gkremo	Cerigo
Moní Agiou Andréa	Cefallonia
Moní Agíou Theodórou	Cerigo
Moni Faneroménis	Levkas
Moní tis Panagías tis Anafonítrias	Zante
Moraïtika	Corfu
Mount Ainos	Cefallonia
Mount Pantokráton	Corfu
Mouzáki	Zante
Mylopótamus	Cerigo
Mýrtou Bay	Cefallonia
Néa Skála	Cefallonia
Nisáki	Corfu
Nisáki	Corfu
Ntouriánika	Cerigo
Nydri	Levkas
Nymfés	Corfu
Palaiochóra	Cerigo
Palaiokastritsa	Corfu
Palaiópoli	Cerigo
Pástra	Cefallonia
Pélekas	Corfu
Perachóri	Ithaca
Peratáta	Cefallonia
Períthea	Corfu
Perivóli	Corfu
Perouládes	Corfu
Pessáda	Cefallonia
Petália	Corfu
Pilikáta	Ithaca
Piso Aetós	Ithaca
Plános	Zante
Platheithiás	Ithaca
Platía Ammos	Cerigo
Pólis Bay	Ithaca

Place Name	Location
Pontikonísi	Corfu
Póros	Cefallonia
Pórto Longós	Paxos
Potamós	Cerigo
Potamós	Corfu
Pyrgí	Corfu
Róda	Corfu
Sámi	Cefallonia
Sidári	Corfu
Sinióri	Cefallonia
Skorpios	Very small island off the east coast of Levkas
Skriperó	Corfu
Sparti	Very small island off the east coast of Levkas
Spartýlas	Corfu
Strongylí	Corfu
Taxiárchis	Ithaca
Tsiliví	Zante
Valaneió	Corfu
Vasilikós	Zante
Vathy	Ithaca
Vátos	Corfu
Vidos	Small island off the east coast of Corfu
Vlacháta	Cefallonia
Vlachérna	Corfu
Volímes	Zante
Ypsos	Corfu
Zóla	Cefallonia

British Cemeteries in the Ionian Islands

Although there were Britons buried in the Ionian Islands as early as 1689[2], and the cemetery at Zante is said to have dated from 1650 where there are some eighteenth century graves, most of the major British cemeteries were of a more recent date. It would appear that the British Cemetery in Corfu dates from at least 1813. It was described in 1896 as 'the picturesque little English cemetery at Corfu, not far behind that under the pyramid of Caius Cestius at Rome in beauty'. There were, in fact, two cemeteries. In one of them there were two Protestant and two Roman Catholic sections, and there was also another small cemetery adjoining the others. They had a total of some 750 graves. The cemeteries overlooked the sea and were at the foot of the walls at the southern end of the Spianata (or Spianádha/Esplanade). The land of the cemeteries has been stated as being 350 yards long by 120 yards wide.

Just before the British departure from the Ionian Islands, the British government opened another cemetery some way from the town – which still survives. Official records state that it was opened 'about 1855' and was confirmed to the British Government in 1863 by a resolution of the Assembly of the Ionian States. This third cemetery (originally known as the Sant Rocco or New British Cemetery) is south of Platía San Rócco, just beyond the Psychiatric Hospital. The area around this cemetery proved to be the site of several other, much earlier, burials, including that of the tomb of the Greek notable, Menekrates, who drowned c.650 BC. (It survives and is now a tourist attraction.) The Sant Rocco cemetery had a curator, James Whitfield, as shown by the Baptism Register for 1866.

In 1890 the British and Greek governments reached an agreement by which the original two cemeteries were handed back to the Corfu municipal authorities who, some twelve years later, leased the site to a Belgian company which constructed a casino. The graves were moved from the old cemeteries to an annexe of the Sant Rocco Cemetery in 1903, under the supervision of the British Vice-Consul, Mr E Vicars. The remains were put into coffins and as they were re-interred at their new site, a vicar was in attendance throughout.

During the move there was much consternation in the British community, and a series of letters were published in *The Times*. When Lord C F Brudenell-Bruce wrote his letter (dated 5 May, published 7 May 1904), describing the insensitive nature of the removal, this was vigorously denied in a letter signed by seven British residents and a further seven who had relations buried in the cemetery. It soon emerged that the Belgian casino company had actually undertaken that the cemetery grounds would become the gardens for the casino, and a nearby site would be used for the actual

---

[2] Sir Clement Harby at Zante.

casino itself. They stated that they had no plans to build gaming rooms over the cemetery.[3]

The transcription of the graves in this volume were made in the early years of the twentieth century (after the graves had been moved). The transcription was made by Otho Alexander, British Vice-Consul at Corfu, and by Arthur F G Leveson Gower (1851-1922), FSA, who sent them to *Miscellanea Genealogica et Heraldica* which published them in 1906-08.[4]

During the First World War there were twelve British soldiers interred at Corfu, and some work was undertaken on restoring some of the earlier graves. However in 1922 the Foreign Office in London were informed that the British cemetery at Cephalonia was much neglected, and they engaged the services of a gardener who was put under the supervision of the British vice-consul.[5]

British Foreign Office reports for 1923 record the supply of headstones for the cemetery at Corfu[6], and in the following year the maintenance of graves in Ionian islands was overhauled, and the cemetery at Zante repaired. A 1927 report notes the maintenance of British cemetery at Cephalonia, and in the next year there were extensive repairs to Cemetery Lodge at Corfu. During the 1930s there were disputes over the use of the wall of British Cemetery at Corfu by Municipal authorities; and also some work on the British cemetery at Cerigo.

Just before the Second World War the graves in the cemetery at Zante were transcribed for the *Genealogists' Magazine*[7] and in about 1939 a new listing was prepared for *Notes & Queries*. The listing was sent to the British Foreign Office but does not appear to have been published by *N&Q*.

A memorial was erected in the surviving Sant Rocco Cemetery in Corfu to the 44 men killed during the Corfu Channel Incident in 1946 when the Albanians attacked two British warships. Some of the men are buried there, whilst others are buried in Malta. That cemetery is still used for civilian burials and is well tended with some wild orchids. The resident gardener, George Psaila, who worked at the cemetery since 1944, was awarded the MBE in 1988 for his conscientious service.

---

[3]   For details on the cemetery see *The Times* 12 March 1896, p10f, 23 May 1896, p7f, 13 Dec 1902, p8a, 12 Sept 1903, p8b, 11 Dec 1903, p8b, 5 May 1904, p10e, 7 May 1904, p18c, 21 May 1904, p8c, 31 May 1904, p15a, 06 June 1904, p6d, 22 June 1904, p6c.

[4]   For Corfu, Paxos etc, see *Miscellanea Genealogica et Heraldica* 4th Series, Vol 1 (1906), p35-38, 68-70, 87-92, 122-25, 195-98, 236-39, 252-56, 311-12; Vol 2 (1908), p13-16, 71-73, 110-12, 146-49, 320-21; 5th Series Vol 8 (1932-34), p85. For Cerigo (Kithira), see 4th Series, Vol 4 (1912), p322-27; for Zante see 4th Series, Vol 5 (1914), p19-27; and for Ithaca see 4th Series, Vol 5 (1914), p177-79.

[5]   1922: K8014/8014/219

[6]   1923: K785/785/219

[7]   *Genealogists' Magazine* Vol 7 (March 1935), p19-21. This listing is a little inaccurate, but where there are differences with existing transcripts, these are noted in squared brackets.

OLD BRITISH CEMETERY, CORFU

1.
>
> To the memory of
> William Edward
> son of
> Captn Sandham, RI Engineers
> and
> Augusta, his wife, who died 27 July
> 1834
> aged 3 months

Charles Sandham, was appointed Second Captain, Royal Engineers on 1 June 1806.

2.
>
> Peter Lamond MD
> Surgeon 2nd Batt, 60th Rifles
> died at Corfu 21 April 1840
> aged 45 years
> This stone is erected to his
> memory by his brother Officers

3.
>
> Cigit
> Nicolays ... Klingenberg
> Premier Lieutenant de la Marine
> Royale Norvegien a Dronthein
> en Norvege le 25 Janvier 1806
> Mort a bord de la Corvette
> Norvegienne L'Ornen
> a Corfu le 21 Novembre
> 1837

4. [Obelisk]

> Sacred
> to the memory of
> Lieutenant Colonel
> William Gardner Freer KH
> who died at Corfu
> Commanding HBM Xth Regiment
> of Infantry on the 2nd August 1836
> aged 45 years
> He served in the 43 Monmouthshire
> Light Infantry, one of the Regiments
> of the Light Division of the Army
> in all Campaigns of the
> Peninsula War from 1808 to 1814
> He was present during that
> eventful period in the Battles
> and Sieges of
> Vimiera, Corunna, Busaco, Fuartes
> d'Onor, Ciudad Rodrigo, Badajos
> Vittoria, Fivelli, Voice, Toulouse
> and lost his right arm at the storming of Badajos
> This tribute to the memory of a
> distinguished soldier
> and sincere friend
> is erected by his brother Officers
>
> Also
> underneath this Monument are
> deposited the remains of
> William Cuming Esqre
> late Lieutenant in HM's 10th Regt of Foot, who died in Corfu the
> 9th of November 1834, aged 25 years.
> His brother officers record and
> lament the untimely fate
> of so amiable a Companion

William Freer was born 27 July 1791 at Coventry and joined the army at the age of fourteen. He was an ensign in the 43rd Foot and then commissioned Lieutenant and then Captain, becoming a Major in 1826. He was in Spain and Portugal during the Peninsular War 1808-14 (losing his arm, amputated after the storming of Badajoz, 6 April 1812), and in France 1817-18. Posted to Gibraltar in 1822-25, he was transferred to the Ionian Islands in July 1828. Gazetted Lieutenant Colonel in 1833, he died at Corfu.

5.
>
> Sacred
> to the memory
> of
> Helen Louisa Weir
> who died
> 21 July 1832
> aged 3 years

6.
>
> Sacred to the memory
> of
> Charles Howse
> Captn's Clerk of HMS *Aigle*
> who died at Corfu
> 9th October 1842, aged 18
> His Shipmates erect this stone
> in memory of one to whose
> musical skill they have
> been indebted for much enjoyment
> in the earnest hope that he
> may have exchanged the vain thing of
> Earth for the Eternal joy of Heaven

The *Aigle* was built in 1801 and decommissioned in 1863, being turned into a coal hulk. It was sunk in shallow water during torpedo experiments at Sheerness and sold to A W Howe.

7.
>
> Sacred to the memory
> of
> Robert Forbes Esqre
> late of Gosport
> who died 19 July 1829
> aged 84

8.

Sacred
to the memory of
McCoolog Crawford
son of Lt Col Crawford
Royal Artillery
and Charlotte, his wife
who departed this life
on the 27th day of August
1827
aged 17 years and 5 months

Also Mr Henry Smart Crawford
late Midshipman on board
HMS *Tweed*
who departed this life
at sea in latitude 3 12 North
Long 9 25 W
on the fifth day of November
1827, aged 15 years, 25 days

9.

In ... memory of
... Marente
...
Lazaretto
died the
... October 1824
[aged] ... years
... this monument was erected
by the Health Officers here
in token of their respect
for a most zealous
... Public Servant

10.

Here
rest the remains of
Georgina
wife of Lt Col Potter
Royal Artillery
She died at the Citadel
on the 10th February 1853
aged 55 years
Thy will be done

11. [Slab with no inscription.]
Lieut Matthews, RA

12.
Sacred
to the memory of
Lord Schomberg Robert Kerr Kt
son to the 6th and brother to the
7th Marquis (sic) of Lothian
Aide de Camp to His Excellency
Sir Frederick Adam and a
Captain in Her Majesty's 32 Regiment
of Foot, who expired at Corfu
on the 12th of August
1825 in the 30th year of his age

Schomberg Robert Kerr was born 15 Aug 1795 at Ancrum, Roxburgh, Scotland; and was baptised 12 Sept 1795 at Newbattle, Midlothian. He was commissioned Captain in the 3rd Regiment. His father, John William Robert Kerr was the 7th Marquess of Lothian and Lord Lieutenant of the county of Roxburgh.

13.
Sacred
to the memory
of
Anna Keightley, infant daughter [of]
Lt Col Keightley, XI Regt and
Anne, his wife. Born the
27 November 1827. Died the
12 April 1828

14.
Sacred
to
the memory of Ensign
George Probyn of His
Majesty's 28 Regt. Son of the
Late Governor Probyn and
Grandson of Edward Probyn Esqre
[of] Newlands in the County of
Gloucester. He departed this life
the 28 day of August 1827
aged 20 years

15.
John Kettlewell
died 29 December 1833
aged 29 years

16. [Red Stone]
Sacred
to the memory of
the honourable Charles Gustavus
Monckton (late) Captain in
HM's 88th Regt (or) Connaught Rangers
who died by the hand of an
assassin on the 9 of August 1831
aged 26 years
This monument
is erected by the non-commissioned
Officers and private soldiers of the
regiment, in testimony of their
respect and regard for this most
lamented young officer, and
to record their abhorrence of the
atrocious act by which he was
deprived of life. The feeling of grief
and indignation, strongly and
universally expressed by the Regiment,
was only moderated on witnessing the prompt
punishment of the murderer
Private James Clark, who was executed
on the 11 of August 1831

Charles Monckton was born 11 May 1806 the second son of the 5th Viscount Galway.

17.
Sacred to the memory of
George Johnstone Esqre
(late)
Surgeon of the 88th Regiment (or Connaught Rangers) who departed this
life on the 8th September 1853, aged 52 years
Erected by his brother Officers as a
testimony of the high esteem in which
he was universally held during
the 22 years he served as Surgeon
in the regiment

18.

Sacred
to the memory of
Eliza Weale
daughter of the deceased
John and Susannah Flack
who
departed this life
the
24th day of April 1840
aged 48 years
This stone was erected by her
disconsolate and loving Husband
as an everlasting tribute of affection
and heartfelt regret for her
premature dissolution
And
Caroline, his second
wife, who died 31st
of October 1848, aged 30

19.

Underneath
are deposed
the mortal remains
of
Donald Munro
Second Lieutenant
and Adjutant
of the
Fifth Fusiliers 1838
Ætat 33
This modest tomb is erected by
the Officers of the Corps as a slight
mark of their high sense of his sterling
worth, of their regards to his memory
& sincere regret of his premature
death

20.
>
> To the memory of
> Colonel Francis Dawkins
> Deputy QrMr and deputy
> Adjt General
> Fourth son of Henry Dawkins
> of Oxford, who died
> April 16th 1847
> aged 50 years

Francis Henry Dawkins was born 4 Oct 1796, and baptised 27 Nov 1796 at Chipping Norton, Oxfordshire, the son of Henry Dawkins and Augusta (née Clinton). He was an officer at the Battle of Waterloo and was serving on the staff in Corfu at his death.

21.
>
> Sacred to the memory of
> Sarah Mary Harcourt
> Third daughter of
> Sir Howard and Lady Douglas
> who departed this life on the 22 of
> November 1835

Sarah's father, Sir Howard Douglas, 3rd Bart, GCB GCMG, FRS, after a distinguished service in the Peninsular War, was gazetted colonel of the 15th Foot. He was Governor of New Brunswick from 1823 to 1829, and was Lord Commissioner of the Ionian Isles from 1835 to 1840. The *Dictionary of National Biography* notes: 'the post was acknowledged to be a difficult one, but despite much misrepresentation at home Douglas governed wisely and well. He foiled conspiracy, domestic and foreign, used his position in the very focus of Russian intrigue to turn his information to the best account, promoted education and public works, and improved the revenue. He introduced a new code of laws based on the Greek model, known as the Douglas Code.' Sir Howard also founded a prize for Ionian College to be given annually. He was later MP for Liverpool from 1842 to 1847. Sir Howard and Lady Douglas had ten children. One son was killed in Afghanistan in 1841, and another died on HMS *Tartar* in the West Indies.

22.
>
> Sacred to the
> memory
> of John Wm Flack
> Died
> the 9th January 18..
> aged 36 years
> This tomb is erected by
> his disconsolate widow

23.

To the memory of
M McPherson, wife of
Lieutenant McPherson, 36th Regiment
died 24 February 1822,
aged 30 years
And also her infant daughter
who died 22 March 1822

24.

M S
Nathaniel, son of Major Scargill
97 Regiment, died 4th July 1844
aged 49 years
His afflicted parents
HMP

25.

Sacred
to the memory of
John William Soper
who departed this life the
22nd day of August
aged 18 months and 13 days
also
John William Soper
his brother
who departed this life on the
16th day of June 1830
aged 13 months and
25 days
Of another sister Sarah, who departed
this life the 6th day of August
1832, aged 3 months and ...
Children of N Soper and Sarah, his wife

26.

XX Do L Do
To
the memory of
John Flack
who died the 8th September 1823
much lamented by
all who knew him
Also
Susanna H Flack
his wife
who departed this life
the 8th March 1837
aged 60 years

27.

Sacred
to the memory of
Nicolas Soper
who departed this life
the 16th year of his age

28.

Sacred
to the memory of
Lieutenant
Alexander Stuart
of the
thirty-second Regiment
who died
August 23, 1823, aged 27 years
This
stone was erected by his
Brother Officers in
testimony of their
Esteem and Regard

29.
Sacred to the memory of
William Petty
Born in Manchester
in the county of Lancaster
October the 30th 1785; died at Corfu
August the 8th 1822; a most
affectionate husband, a tender
father and a sincere friend

He was possibly William, son of William Pattey (sic) who was baptised 27 Nov 1785 at Manchester Cathedral.

30. [Red Stone]
Sacred
to the memory of
John Hile Parsons
of Parson
CGM Lt Col in Her Britannic
Majesty's Service and 21 years
Resident to the Lord High
Commissioner of the Ionian Islands
Died at Corfu on the 20th April
1848, in the 63 year of his age
Deeply lamented by all
who knew him

31.
Sacred
to the memory
of
John Carew Brown
Midshipman
of
H Majesty's ship *Redpoer*
who departed this life at the
early aged of 14 years

32.
Sacred to the memory
of
Lieutenant Henry Ogle, 36 Regiment
who departed this life in the
Island of Corfu
The 13th of December 1821
aged 46 years
He was a kind Father
an affectionate Husband
and a sincere friend.
The just Man walketh in his
integrity, and his children are
blessed after Him.
This has been erected by his wife

33.

H O

34.
Sacred to the memory of
Captain David Craigie
97 Regiment
aged 30 years, son of
George Clarke Craigie Esqre
Dumarnie House,
Perthshire
who died after two days' illness
on the 19 February 1844, deeply
regretted by his friends [and]
brother officers

35.
Sacred
to the memory of
Captain Robert Lisle
Late of the 97th Regiment
who died on the 15th November 1843
aged 37 years
This stone is erected by
His brother officers

36.

Sacred
to the memory of
Susannah
wife of Colonel John Hassard
Royal Engineers
who departed this life on the
3 March 1833, in her
fifty-fourth year
Also of Susannah, daughter
of the above, who died the
13th February 1837, in the
25th year of her age

John Hassard was commissioned Captain, Corps of Royal Engineers, on 20 July 1804, and promoted to Major on 18 Nov 1807.

37.

Sacred
to the memory of
Lieut H Harris Scobell
HP, Late 95 Regiment
who departed this life
on the 19 November 1854
aged 23 years
Erected by His Brother
Officers, who deeply deplore
the untimely fate of this amiable
young man

38.

Here
lyeth the remains of
Edward Johnson Esqre
Ensign in the 51st (of the King's Own)
Light Infy Regiment
who died November 10th 1822
aged 23 years
To whose memory his Brother Officers
caused this monument
to be erected

39.
Sacred
to the memory of
Thomas Rattray Blair
son of
Assistant Comm General Ramsay
and
Martha, his wife
on the 28th January 1833
aged 13 years

40.
Sacred
to the memory of
Louisa Jane, daughter of
Assistant Staff Surgeon Trigance
aged 3 years, 89 days
Died on the 22
March 1830

41.
Hic
Pulvis jacet
Qui nuper vixit
Non sine pectore corpus
Ricardus Edmundus Scott
Praefectus artificium horum
militarium Vernacunis qui
Royal Engineers dicuntur
Sub Rege Imperii conjuncti
Magnae Britanniae Hiberniaeque &c
Juvenis
Animo fuit probus, inginieque
orratus. In studiis
Quibuscunque honestis non
incultus, Sed arte in sua propria
Paecipae edoctus
Quam acriter plus aequopersequentem
Adoperatumque exequi chartam
Rei militaris in usum
Insulae Corcyrae
Lethatis incantum corripuit
Febris maligno exorta caelo
Natus in Comitatu Bedfordiae
Carus vixit amicus

42.

>
> Sacred
> to the memory of
> Ann Charlotte
> infant daughter of
> Major J W Parsons ADC
> and Mary Elisabeth, his wife
> aged fourteen months

John Whitehill Parsons, was commissioned Captain on 3 Dec 1805.

43.

>
> Sacred
> to the memory of
> Peter J Macdonald Esqre
> Apothecary to the Forces
> who died February 4th 1829
> aged 88 years

44.

>
> Sacred
> to the memory of
> Alfred Macdonald [?Lawrence]
> son of ...
> Lieut ...
> 32 Regiment
> Born in the Island of Guernsey
> 29 December 1816
> Died at Corfu 4th August 1819
> aged 2 years & 4 months

Samuel Hill Lawrence, the probable father, was commissioned Captain, 32nd Regt, on 10 Nov 1807.

45.

This tablet
The last sad tribute of
affection is consecrated to the
memory of Geraldine Frances
D'Aguilar, wife of George Bradford
Ellicombe Esqre
who died in this Island
on the 19th of March 1848, aged 28
Also of
Charles Ford
The only child of the above
who died in England on the
18th of April 1847
aged four months
I will ransom them from the power
of the Grave, I will redeem them
from death Hos 14

46.

In a vault
near this stone are deposed the
remains of Sarah, the wife of
Major Brandreath of the Royal Artillery
who died beloved and lamented
October 18th 1819, aged 35 years
Also of Sarah Jane, her new born infant
who died at the same time

Thomas A Brandreath was commissioned Captain, Royal Regt of Artillery, 20 Dec 1804.

47.

D O M
Mary Lauder (or Lander)
died at Corfu 18 February 1846
aged 94 years

Mary Lauder [or Lander] & Sarah Brandreath

48.

Sacred
to the memory of
Lieut Edward Stephens
32nd Regiment
who died 29th March 1819
aged 27 years
This monument was erected
by his brother Officers
as a testimony
of their esteem and regret

49.

Sacred
to the memory of
Charlotte Anne, daughter
of William & Bridget Bingham
She died the 28th of July 1819
aged 3 years and 7 months
Of such is the Kingdom of God

50.

To the memory of
Major General Haviland Smith
Commanding the Garrison of this Island
who
after having served His Majesty
with honour to himself
and credit to his country
for a term of 34 years in
Brabant, Holland, France, Egypt, Italy
and Spain
and in a civil capacity as
Governor of Zante and the other
Ionian islands, then under the British
in which services he united in an eminent degree the firm character of the
Soldier with the amiable snavity
of the Gentleman
Closed his glorious career
26 of February 1817
in the 44 year of his age
Universally
respected, beloved, regretted
This stone may give a slight sketch of
the merits of the lamented Officer
A far fuller portrait remains
indelibly engraved on
the hearts of all who knew him

Haviland Smith was appointed Ensign in the 57th Foot and commissioned Lieutenant in an independent company in 1790. During the early years of the Napoleonic Wars he served with the Marines in the Mediterranean and after the landing at Toulon he raised an independent company of Chasseurs. Upon their evacuation from Toulon he was attached to the emigrant corps in England, and then served with the Corsican Corps. Taking part in the Egyptian Campaign, he also saw action in Sicily. Gazetted Colonel in 1810, he became a Major-General in 1813.

51.

Sacred
to the memory of
William Cartwright Esqre
Late collector of Customs
in the Island of Corfu
who died on the 8th December
1841

52.

Sacred to
the memory of
Isabella Mary Anne Bertie,
daughter of
Thomas I L, Captain HM's X Reg, Galloway
and Isabella Ann, his wife
who died at Corfu xi July,
aged 21 months
Also
their infant son
William Frances
who died at Corfu
October 3rd 1850
[aged] ... and .. months

53.

Sacred
to the memory of
Captain
John Brydge Leonard
of the
Thirty-second Regiment
who died
August 3rd 1819, aged 22 years
This
stone was erected by his
Brother Officers
in
Testimony of their esteem and regret
and
Mary Sofia, their daughter, who
[died] ... January 1831
... months
... This stone ... not my mouth of ...

54.

No inscription surviving

55.
>
> Sacred
> to the memory of
> Lieut George Pigot
> 90th Light Infantry
> who departed this life 23 April 1830
> aged 28 years
> This monument is erected
> by his Brother officers as a mark
> of their esteem and deep regret at
> his early death

Possibly George, the eldest son of Sir George Pigot, 3rd Bart.

56.
>
> Wee Pitsey
> 1841

57.
>
> Here are deposited
> the remains of
> Mr Robert Reid
> son of
> Robt Reid Esqre
> of Tullirge in Kinross-shire,
> Scotland, who died on the 25
> of July 1818, in the ...
> year of his age

58.
>
> Near this place lie the remains
> of Mary Davies
> the wife of Captain John Davies
> Royal Artillery
> and also daughter of the late
> Henry Hickman Esqre
> of Newham in the County
> of Northampton
> who died the 12 April 1830
> aged 28 years
> Also Mary, daughter of the above
> who departed this life
> the 29th December 1829
> aged 34 years

59.
Sacred
to the memory of
Jane Maria Theresa Townsend
wife of L Co Adjt Townsend
2nd Battn 60 Rifles
who departed this life
on the 6th December 1839
aged 30 years
Also her infant daughter
who died 14th July 1839
aged 4 months

60.
Sacred
to the memory of

61.
Sacred
to the memory of
Cosmo George Frederick
5th son of Major-General Sir Alexander
& Lady Woodford, born at Genova (sic)
the 17 July 1830, died at Corfu
26th June 1833
to the inexpressible grief of his parents
In the same Grave are likewise deposited
the remains of
Gordon
the infant son of Sir Alexander
and Lady Woodford
Born at Corfu July 12th 1833, died the
20th of the same month

Sir Alexander Woodford was the elder son of Lieut-Col John Woodford and his second wife Susan, eldest daughter of Cosmo George, third Duke of Gordon. Alexander was born in London in 1782, attended Winchester College and obtained a commission as an ensign in 1794, and was commissioned Lieutenant in the following year. He saw action during the Napoleonic Wars in the Coldstream Guards and joined the staff of Lord Forbes in Sicily, before rejoining the Coldstream Guards during the Peninsular Wars. He commanded the 2nd Battalion of the Guards at Waterloo and was then a part of the occupation force in France. Posted to Malta in 1825, two years later he was transferred to Corfu where he was, in 1832, appointed to command the British forces in the Ionian Islands and acted as temporary High Commissioner. He married Charlotte Mary Ann Fraser, daughter of the British Minister at Hamburg. A son, Charles, was killed leading a charge at Cawnpore during the Indian Mutiny and is commemorated in a stained glass window at Westminster Abbey.

62.

Lieut Jelicoon
HMS *Sybille*

63.

Near this wall are deposited
the remains of Emilie Lanpetta Powell
the daughter of Lieut-Col Keyt
of the 51st or King's Own Light Infantry
who died on the 10 of August 1823
aged 13 months

64.

Alfred Buckton
Mitchison
son of Thomas R Mitchison
Assist Com General
& Harriet, his wife
Died
11 June 1839
aged 3 years and 65 days

65.

Thomas R Mitchison
Assist Commissary General
died 6th April 1842
aged 56 years

66.

Frederick Baillie
Staff Assistant Surgeon
Died 9th April 1846
Aged 28 years

67.

DOM
Sacred to the memory of
Caroline Amelia Forrest
wife of Robert Forrest Esqre
Member of the Supreme Council of
Justice in the Ionian Islands
who departed this life
on the iv day of March
AD MDCCCXXVII
aged xlviii (48)
Also of
Robert Forrest Esqre
who departed this life
on the xxviii
of February
AD MDCCCXXXIII
Aged
lxxii

68.

Sacred
to the memory of
Harriet Browne Pecco
wife of
Acct Cr Gl Christopher Pecco
deceased 8 July 1865
aged 34 years
Deeply regretted for her estimable Qualities
as daughter, wife and parent
Ei Acmutae
Frumteir Frunestyr

69.
Sacred
to the memory of
Anne Mary Brown
daughter of Lieut Brown RA
and Eleanor, his wife
Died 24 June 1829
aged 4 months
Also
To the memory of
Charles Henry Crawford Br[own]
their second child, who died
October 16, 1830, aged 7 months

70.
To the memory of
Susanna Maria Wilhelmina
only daughter of
F Fanenan Esqre ...
Aged ... years and 4 months

71.
Sacred
to the memory of
Lieut John Trevor Hull
48 Regt
Formerly of 18 Royal Irish
who departed this life
at Corfu 22nd March 1825
aged 29 years
This stone was erected by
his Brother Officers of the 18 Royal Irish Regt
as a token of their esteem and regard

72.

Sacred
to the memory of
...
infant ...
[of]
Captain Adair ? [?]
...th Regiment
who departed this life at Corfu
the one of the ... June 1817
aged 1 month, 10 days
the other on the 12 August 1819
aged 1 year and 2 months
Of such is the Kingdom of Heaven
Also
Alfred McGregor Adair [?Andain]
aged 5 month and 17 days

The surname was transcribed as Andain but may have been Adair. However the officer was most probably either Lieut James Adair or Lieut Robert Adair. There was also a Lieut Johann Hein Adair, 60th Royal American Regt.

73.

Sacred to the memory
of
Harriet, daughter of
George and Olivia Lonon Conyngham
and wife of Major Portlock RE
who departed February 23rd 1817
aged 18
Characterized in health by
a pure, gentle, truthful, and consistent spirit
She was prepared to enter into that rest
which is reserved for the faithful in Christ Jesus

74.

To mark
where rest the remains of
one of the most affectionate wives
and
best of mothers
Eleonor R Uniake
wife of Wm Hacket Esqre MD
Deputy Inspector General
Died April 19, 1849
aged 50 years

75.

To the memory of
James
son of
Denzil and Martha Ibbeston [?Ibbetson]
Died 20th July 1832
aged 21 weeks
Also
to his niece
Eliza Emily Bubina
daughter of
Fred H Ibbetson
Dep Asst Comy General
who died
on the 16th March 1850, aged 3 months and
3 weeks
The Lord gave and the Lord hath taken away. Blessed be the name of the Lord

76.

To mark
where rest the remains of
Captain R Hacket H P
who died at Corfu, July 13th 1848
aged 63 years
He served throughout Peninsula War
with his Regiment the 7th Royal Fusiliers
and also at the attack on
New Orleans

77.

Sacred
to the memory of
Louisa Maria
and
Jno Frederick O'Reilly
infant children of B O'Reilly Esqre
Paymaster of the 18th Royal Irish Regiment
and of Mary his wife

78.
Near this spot
lies the remains of
Lieut I E Thomson, 18th Regiment
who departed this life
on the
6th April 1830
This stone is erected as a testimony of the regard
and esteem of his Brother Officers

II

1.
To the memory of
Sarah Kind
who departed this life, 13 February
1844, aged 24 years
Also
her daughter Jane
who died
21 January 1842
1 year and 7 months

2.
Sacred
to the memory of
Thomas William
son of Thomas Kind, Band Master
of the 17 Regiment
who died 21 August 1851
aged
1 year, 11 months

3.
Isaac Brown

4.
Thomas Weagan

5.

Sacred
to the memory of
Elias Laseter
late Rope maker
to HMS *Inconstant* who died July
7th 1845
This stone was erected
by his mess mates
as a token of Esteem

6.

George Webber

7.

[In] memory of Sergt I Keating

8.

Sacred
to the memory
of
John McCallum
of the Corps of Royal Sappers
& Miners
who departed this life on
the 11th day of August 1813
aged 28 years

John McCallum was commissioned Lieutenant on 18 Oct 1803.

9.

Sacred
to the memory
of
Richard Williams (Sapper
& Miner)
who departed this life
the 9th day of September
aged 20 years

10.

To the memory of
David Jenkins, Royal Sappers
& Miners, who died May 1st 1820
aged 32 years
Also his son David Jenkins of the
9th Compy Royal Sappers & Miners
who departed this life Dec^ber 23 1838,
aged 25 years

11.

Sacred
to the memory
of
Samuel Ashton

12.

Sacred
to the memory of
David Marshall
late Private in the 6th Company
Royal Sappers and Miners
whose death was occasioned
by a stone from a Blast
which killed him on the
spot on the island of Vido
on the 14 of July 1826 in the 26
year of his age

13.

[Illegible]
Sappers

14.

Sacred
to the memory of
John Allen
Paymaster Serjeant of the 4th Regt
who departed this life August 7th 1850
aged 35 years
This stone is erected by his comrade Serjeants
as a token of their esteem and regard

15.
>
> Sacred to the
> Memory of
> Margaret Taylor
> wife of James Taylor
> who departed this life
> 8 day of November 1851
> aged 70 years
> This is erected by her son as a
> token of filial affection

16.
>
> Sacred
> to the memory
> of
> James Taylor
> who departed this life
> on the 18 November 1841

17.
>
> Sacred
> to the memory
> of
> Mary Quinland
> eldest daughter of
> James and Margaret Taylor
> who departed this life
> 1 September 1845

18.
>
> Sacred
> to the memory of
> Wilhelmina Quinland
> daughter of Charles and Elizabeth Quinland
> Born 8 July 1861
> Died 9 July 1865

19.

Sacred
to the memory of
Frederick G Taylor
who departed this life
September 2nd 1849
aged 11 months

20.

Sacred
to the memory of
Henrietta M Taylor who
departed this life
January 2nd, 1857, aged 6 years

21.

Sacred
to the memory
of
Elizabeth Jameson
who departed this life 24 March 1821
aged 11 years

22.

Sacred
to the memory
of
William and Eliza Hickson
son & daughter of James & Mary Hickson
28 & 6 years of age, who departed
this life on the 28 July and 6 Dec[ber]
1819

23.

To the
memory of
Mary Clough
daughter of Towers & Mary Clough
who departed this life
October 23 1828, aged
1 year, 11 months

24.
>
> To the
> memory of
> John Masterton
> who departed this life
> on the 26th day of
> December 1842
> aged 51 years

25.
>
> Sacred
> to the memory of
> Frances Harris
> daughter of John & Elizabeth Harris
> of the Royal Artillery
> who departed
> this life the 16th day of June 1849
> aged one year

26.
>
> Catherine, wife to
> Thomas Weagar
> 47 years

27.
>
> Sacred
> to the memory of
> Thomas Bozard
> Born at Bath in the County of
> Somersetshire, England, who
> departed this life on the 5th Decr 1817
> aged 25 years
> This stone was erected by Thomas
> Hart, Sapper-Paymaster of the
> 32 Regiment

28.

Sacred
to the memory of
Serjeant J Ross
late of the 18 RIR
died 33 years of age
& of Mary, his wife E [sic], 27 years
both of whom departed this life
within a few weeks of each other
in September 1828

29.

Sacred
to the memory of
M George Johnston, Merchant a
native of Edinborough [sic], who died at
Corfu on the 13th day of July 1822
aged 34 years

30.

Sacred
to the memory of
Catherine Adams, who died 19 May 1822
aged 6 years & 6 months

31.

Sacred
to the memory of
Thomas Mitchell
who died 8th December 1852
aged 20 years

32.

To the memory
of Gunner & Driver
Henry Soper of the 1 Batt
Royal Artillery

33.

Sacred
to the memory of
John Wild
Gunner & Driver
M No 5 Company, 1st Battalion
who departed this life on the 15th day
of July 1849, aged 24 years
This memorial is erected by
the men of the company as a
token of respect for their deceased comrade

34.

Eleanor Sheppard

35.

Sacred
to the memory of
William Henry Pepporall
aged 16 months
who departed this life
the 4th of October AD 1817

36.

John Dugan

37.

W C Wasey
DACC

38.

Sacred
to the memory of
H I & [sic] Davis
Store Keeper
in the
Commissariat
who died at Corfu
on the 9th April 1842, aged 53 years

39.
Sacred
to the memory of
Matilda Anne Bernard
the much beloved daughter of
Augusto and Mary Bernard
who departed this life on the 2 June 1855
aged 4 years & 5 months
Gone but not lost

40.
Sacred
to the memory of
Sarah, wife of
...

41.
Sacred
to the memory of
Ellen Esther & Eugine
infant children of
Matthew and Anna Page

42.
Sacred
to the memory of
Matthew Page
who departed this life
October 12th 1861
Aged 77 years

43.
To the memory of
Samuel Sheard
late Serjeant Major
34th Regt
who died at Corfu
5 November 1849
aged 32 years
This stone was erected by his Brother
NC Offs as a token of respect

44.

Sacred
to the memory of
Henry Rabling
late Serjeant in the 51 or King's Own L
Infantry Regiment
who died on the 26 day of
November 1828
Aged 47 years

45.

The mortal remains
of Donald Steward, late
Quartermaster of the 88th Regt, are
interred in this place
He died on the 10th February 1881

46.

Sacred
to the memory of
Capt Josh Stainton
who died at Corfu
on the 28 October
1832

47.

In memory
of
Mark Ann Mennice
who died 26th Jany 1846
aged 7 years and 2 months

48.

Arthur Gilpin
died 4th of October 1830
aged 12 days
Edward William Gilpin
died 6 December 1830, aged 19 months

49.

Sacred
to the memory of
George, son of Joseph and Caterina Marshall
who died 17th March 1859
aged 6 weeks

50.

Here lies the body
of
George Lucton
by birth a Scotchman
Late Serjeant
in HBM's 75 Regt of Foot
He was an agreeable companion,
a good soldier, & a faithful friend
but alas
on the 4th day of August
1816, he was cut off by the hand of an
assassin in the 24th year of his age
As a mark of sincere esteem this
stone is consecrated to his
memory by his brother Serjeants
24 May AD 1817

51.

This tablet is erected
by the Non Commd Officers & Privates
of the Light Compy 36th Regiment as a
tribute of Respect to the under-mentioned
men who departed this life in the Ionian Islands from 1847 to 1851
Serjeant Edward Mills
Lc Sergt Charles Fairey
Pte Thomas Carry
Pte William Day
Pte James Hall
Pte George Hargrave
Pte James McJarlin

52.

                  Sacred to the memory of
the undermentioned men of No ... Compy
5th Regiment, Royal Artillery
who died in the Ionian Islands from
March 1843 to April 1849
Corporal Wm Rewes   Aged 40, at Corfu
Bombd Urb Downing   Aged 34, at Zante
Bombd Jas Wilson   Aged 24, at Cephalonia
Bombd Jas Thomson   Aged 24, at Corfu
Bombd Thos Garland   Aged 20, at Corfu
Bombd Robert Bell   Aged 33, at Corfu
This stone is erected by their Brother
Non-Commd Officers & Gunners to perpetuate
their memory and to mark in a form ...
We mourn not as men without hope for those who die in the Lord

53.

Sacred
to the memory of
Willoughby Clement Wasey Esqre DAOG
who died much lamented at Corfu
September the 27th 1840
of a remittent fever caught in the
discharge of his duty at Cephalonia
aged 28 years

54.

Sacred
to the memory of
Alexander Frances Ogilvie
son of Co Serjt Thomas Gibson
5th Battn Royal Artillery
who died at Corfu
5th September 1846
aged 99 days

III
Roman Catholic Section

1.

Erected by Elizabeth Numan
to the memory of her beloved
husband John Numan, Master
Tailor, 76th Regiment,
who departed this life April 18th 1849
aged 43 years
Also her infant daughter
Anne Agnes Numan
who departed this life July 28th 1848
aged 3 months
May he rest in peace, Amen

2.

Sacred
to the memory of
John Barry, son of Garrett & Eliza Barry
who departed this life September the
11th 1841
aged 11 years

3.

Sacred
to the memory of
Private Timothy Calvin, late of the
97th Regt, who departed this life
April 8, 1844
aged 40 years
leaving a widow and four sons
to lament his death
Also his daughter, Sarah Calvin,
who died Octr 6th 1843
This stone was erected by his family
as a token of respect to their remains

4.
In excelsis Deo Gloria
Sacred to the
memory of the late
Gunners & Drivers Patrick Ward
who died 20 July 1844, aged 21 years
and Richard Green, who died 15 August
1844, aged 21 years
This stone was erected by their
Comrades of No One Company 5th Battn
Royal Artillery as a deserved token of
regard and esteem

5.
Mary Agnes Woods
the beloved daughter of
William and Mary Woods
46th Regt, who departed this life
the 12th July 1838,
aged 9 months

6.
Sacred to the
memory of
P Bodie, late Serjt 28 Regt
who departed this life on the 14th September 1824
aged 31 years

7.
In memory of the children
of John and Mary Hardy
Royal Artillery
To Mary who departed this life on the
31st January 1855, aged 8 years, 7 months
and John on the 11 March 1855,
aged 5 years & 21 days

8.

Sacred
to the memory of
Thomas Cachill
son of Color Serjeant Patrick Cachill
19th Regt
who died on the 1st October 1852
aged 9 months

9.

Hughes

10.

By
William Gant, 2nd Batt 60 Rifles
in memory of his son James who died
Novr 1840, aged 10 years

11.

Sacred
to the memory of
Daniel Coveney
Serjeant Vth Fusiliers
who died 27th January 1842
aged 34 years

12.

In memory of
Mary Ann McDonald, daughter
of James & Anne McDonald, 32 Regt
who died the 2 Novr 1823,
aged 2 months

13.

Sacred to the memory of
John McGineley
Gunner and Driver
in No 3 Company
1st Battalion
Royal Artillery
who departed this life on the
14 January 1852, aged 23 years

14.

Elizabeth Hammick
wife of
Corporal John Hammick
3 Company, Royal Sappers & Miners
who departed this life 23 March 1851,
aged 28 years
Also of
John Hammick, his son
who died 15 Novr 1848, aged 12 months
Requiescat in Pace
Amen

15.

Sacred
to the memory of
William Hurley Esqre
who departed this life
14 March
1825, aged 25

16.

To
the memory of
James Hughes
who departed this life
the 8 July 1822
aged 6 years

17.

Sacred
to the memory of
Peter Bingham
who departed this life on the
16th February 1827
Also
Elizabeth Bingham, his wife
who departed this life 7th September 1839
aged 60 years

18.

Sacred
to the memory of
Owen Rafferty
son of George
who departed this life on the
10th August 1839,
aged 9 years

19.

Sacred
to the memory of
Patrick Clark
Serjt, Grenadier Company
30th Regt
who departed this life
12 June 1829
aged 35 years

20.

Sacred
to the memory of
Serjt P Conway
97 Regiment
who departed this life
August 26th 1845
aged 22 years
Also
Serjt William Molloy
of the same Corps
who departed this life
Octr 6th 1843
aged 37 years

21.

To
the memory
of Joseph Quanley
son of
Serjeant Major
Thomas S Quanley
97th Regiment
who departed this life
on the 12th February 1845
aged 13 months

22.
>
> Sacred
> to the memory of
> Margaret Smith
> daughter of Frederick Smith
> who departed this life
> on the 21 March 1845
> aged 13

23.
>
> To the memory of
> John Hart, late Musician
> in the 9th Regt, who departed this life
> on the 26 day of December 1830,
> aged 16 years

24.
>
> Sacred
> to the memory of
> Robert White
> who departed this life
> on the 5th May 1837
> aged 26

25.
>
> Sacred
> to the memory of
> Michael Burke, late
> Private Soldier, 51th (sic) King's Own Light Infantry
> who departed this life on the
> 7th day of February 1884
> aged 38 years

26.

Sacred
to the memory of
Catherine
the beloved
wife
of
Assist Commissary General
I W Reid
who departed this life on
the 7th of May
in the 46 year of her
age

27.

Sacred
to the memory of
Margaret Rooney,
wife of Serjeant Rooney
Royal Artillery
who was suddenly called to a better world
immediately after child birth
on the morning of the
2nd July 1855,
aged 28 years

28.

To the memory of
John Charles Gillegan
died January 28, 1851
aged 4 years

29.

DOM
AEmilio
Puero Amantissimo
Johannes Bestardus et Theresia Cologan
Parentes
in dilectionis moerorisque Tesseram
Lacrimis Pulvere
vixit menses VIII Dies XXV
Natus 4°, Obiit 28° Kal Marth
1848

30.
>Gloria in Excelsis Deo
>†
>IHS
>Sacred to the memory of
>James Nowlan, son to Colour Serjeant
>John Nowlan of the XIth Regiment Infantry
>who departed this life on the 7th of May
>1829, aged 7 weeks

31.
>Sacred
>to the memory of
>Catherine,
>wife to Quarter Master Serjeant
>Thos Grady, 51 Regt,
>who departed this life
>the 28th of May 1855
>aged 36 years
>Requescat in Pace
>Amen

32.
>†
>IHS
>Sacred
>to the memory of
>Theresa, wife of
>Serjeant MacSweeney
>of the 9th Regt, who died
>on the 21st July 1815
>aged 34 years

33.
>Sacred
>to the memory of
>Mich C M MacSweeney
>Colour Serjeant of the 97th Regiment
>who died 18 October 1815

Surname for nos 32 and 33 as transcribed.

34.

Sacred
to the memory of
Owen McCabe
who died at Corfu
8 November 1845,
aged 45 years

35.

Sacred
to the memory of
Eleonor,
wife of William Campatan, Private
Soldier of the 10th Regiment of Foot
who departed this life in child bed (sic)
on the 10th day of April 1837,
aged 34 years

36.

Sacred
to the memory of
Private John Connors
No 3 Company 3rd Foot, the Buffs
who died 29th January 1857

37.

Sacred
to the memory of
Private John Callagan, 77 Regiment
who departed this life 28th August 1842

38.
S
I † H
R
I † N
J
Sacred
to the memory of
Elizabeth,
daughter of
William and Sarah Anne Mavin
who departed this life
18th September 1850, aged 4 years
and 9 months

39.
†
Sacred
to the memory of
Martha Louisa
daughter of
Quartermaster Serjeant & Margaret
Liebreith
who died November 9th 1855

40.
Sacred
to the memory of
Mary, wife of Corp Nicolas
Connor of the 88th Foot
who departed this life on the
6th December 1832, aged 27 years

41.
Sacred
to the memory of
John Swann, died 8th April 1833
Mary Murrey, died 12th September 1857
Francis John Swann, died 6th August 1845
Adelaide Swann, died 26 April 1849
Louisa Swann, died 13 July 1850

42.

Sacred
to the memory of Private Luke
McNiel of the XI Regt of Infantry who departed
this life on the Xth day of July 1828, aged 38 years

43.

Sacred
to the memory of
Edward Purdell
Late Quarter Master Serjeant
of the Regt Battn 99 Foot
who departed this life 5th December
1841
aged 37 years

44.

Sacred
to the memory of
Ellen Hewson
wife of Col Serjeant Michael Hewson
49 Regt
who departed this life
25 December 1851
aged 33 years

45.

This tablet
is erected by the Non Commd Officers &
Privates of the Light Company 36 Regiment
as a tribute of respect to the undermentioned
men who departed this life in the
Ionian Islands from 1847 to 1850
Pte John Cutterson
Pte James Logan
Pte James Shinners

IV

1.

Sacred
to the memory of
Quarter master Edward Collins
late of the 36 Regiment who
departed this life on the 21 January
1818, 22 years of age

2.

Sacred
to the memory of
Corporal Thomas Walman
76 Regiment, who departed this life
July the 2nd 1849, aged 24 years
also
his daughter, Emily Ann,
aged one year and four months

3.

Illegible

4.

Sacred
to the memory of
Bombmr Joseph Barr
Company 17 Battery, Royal Artillery
who departed this life 1851
aged 21 years

5.

Adeline Baker

6.

Sacred
to the memory of
Harriet Hall,
daughter of Gunner C Hall
9th Battn, Royal Artillery
who died at Corfu, 27 July 1853,
aged 1 year, 9 months

7.
>
> Sacred
> to the memory of
> Gunner & Driver James Goodall
> No 6 Compy, 9th Battn Royal Artillery
> who died at Corfu 11th July 1803 (sic),
> aged 24 years

8.
>
> Sacred
> to the memory of
> Gunner & Driver Wm Grace
> No 6 Compy, 9th Battn Royal Artillery
> who died at Corfu 2nd January 1853,
> aged 25 years

9.
>
> Sacred
> to the memory of
> Mary Muspratt,
> late wife of
> Color Serjt Henry Muspratt
> 80 Regiment
> who departed this life
> 10 June 1829
> aged 32 years

10.
>
> Sacred
> to the memory of
> Frances Baker
> died 11 May 1847
> 31 years of age

11.
>
> Mary Murray

12.

Sacred
to the memory of
John Hossack,
Private Soldier, HM's 2nd Royal
Highlanders, who departed this life
on the 6th December 1836,
aged 41 years

13.

Sacred
to the memory of
William Hamer
Late Private
Light Company 80th Regiment
who unfortunately lost his life
while bathing at Vido
29 June 1829,
aged 36 years

14.

Sacred
to the memory of
Gunner & Driver
Richard Byers
No 6 Company, 9th Regiment
Royal Artillery
who died at Corfu 26 May
1853
aged 37 years
Also
Thomas McRoberts
who was drowned at sea
the 10th of September 1851
This stone is erected by the Company
as a token of respect

15.

Sacred
to the memory of
Mary Anne and John
the children of Color Serjeant
MacKinlay
and Elizabeth, his wife

16.

Illegible

17.

Illegible

18.

Illegible

19.

Sacred
to the memory of
Gunner and driver
Edward Ashmore
No 6 Company, 9th Regiment
Royal Artillery
who departed this life at Corfu
20 November 1853
aged 41 years
This stone was erected by his company

20.

Sacred
to the memory of
Joseph Hancock
late Chief Warder
of the Military Prison
at Vido
who died 10 September 1851,
aged 42 years

21.

Sacred
to the memory of
Gunner and Driver William Skinner
No 6 Company, 9 Regiment
who died at Corfu on the
5 August 1850,
aged 27 years and nine months

22.

Sacred
to the memory of
John Edward, son of
John and Lydis McLain
who died on the 8th February 1858
3 years, 2 months

23.

Sacred
to the memory of
Fanny Maria King,
daughter of Color Serjeant
John and Elizabeth King, R Artillery
who died September 1819, aged 2 years
7 months

24.

Sacred
to the memory of
Private David Salter, D Company, 77th Regt
who departed this life 16 August 1842
aged 32 years
This stone was erected by his comrades of D Comy as a token of respect

25.

Sacred
to the memory of the undermentioned
erected by No 5 Co 2nd Battn R Artillery

	Aged	Died
Bombar John Earwaker	24	1852
Gunner Wm Brinker	28	1852
Gunner Wm Wallace	30	1853
Gunner Wm Merriman*	19	1854
Gunner George Bankaw*	29	1855
Gunner Geo Lambert*	28	1855
Gunner George Spence	21	1856
Gunner Robert Allan	34	1851
Gunner John Simpson †	23	1851
Gunner Saml Wilson †	22	1851
Gunner Willm Travers ‡	37	1852
Gunner Richd Claridge ‡	28	1854
Gunner Walter Lindsay	20	1856
Gunner Denis Robinson	20	1856

Company embarked for England 1856

* Killed in the trenches, Crimea
† Drowned at Corfu
‡ Died at Zante

26.

Sacred
to the memory of
Gunr and Driver William Ferguson, No 6 Compy
9 Battn, Royal Artillery, who departed this life at Corfu
22nd July 1852
aged 39 years
This stone was erected by the Company
as a token of respect

27.

Sacred
to the memory of
Gunr & Driver Adam Wright
No 6 Compy 9 Battn Royal Artillery
who died at Corfu 19th May 1852
aged 37 years
This stone was erected by the Company
as a token of respect

28.

Sacred
to the memory of
John Rutherford
2nd Battn 60 King's Royal Rifles
who departed this life 12th Febry 1839
aged 27 years
No more his brethren, kind and bright,
Shall him invest with honours grand
No more he'll learn the rules of right
That guide to night the sacred hand (sic)
This stone was erected by the Society he
was a member of as a slight mark of
their esteem and regret for his
premature death

29.

Leaky [Leahy]

30.

Sacred
Amicitia Amor et Veritas
To the memory of
William Cummins No 2 Compy
7th Battn Royal Artillery
who departed this life 2 April 1840
aged 37 years
This stone was erected by the Society
he was a member of as a mark of their
esteem and regret for his premature death

31.

Sacred
to the memory of
David Robertson
...

32.

Sacred
to the memory of
Jemina Roberts,
the beloved wife of
Gunner Jacob Roberts
Royal Artillery
who departed this life
at Vido
on the 12 Novr 1855, aged 29 years
Also
to his beloved son Edward Roberts
who departed this life
on the 21 March 1855
aged 1 year and 9 months

33.

Sacred
to the memory of
Color Serjeant Alexander Small
of the 6th Battn Royal Artillery
who died on the 28th July 1830
aged 37 years

34.

Sacred
to the memory of
Robert Smith
Gunner and Driver in No 5 Company
who departed this life
31 March 1851,
aged 36 years
This memorial was erected by the
Men of his Company as a token
of respect

35.

Sacred
to the memory of
William Abraham Brown
who departed this life the
23 of February 1829
aged 40 years
And
of Elisabeth his wife
who departed this life
the 24 October 1830
aged 40 years

36.

Sacred
to the memory of
the late Bombardier R C Mear [Mears]
No 6 Company, 9th Battn Royal Artillery
who died at Corfu 2nd July 1853
aged 17 years & 2 months
Much beloved and deeply regretted
by all his comrades
whose last tribute of esteem for
those virtues is here given
which distinguished him as a
Soldier, endeared him as a son
and made him a valued friend
of those who while they can lament
his loss, would honour his memory

37.

Sacred
to the memory of
John Paterson
Master of the *School of Hope*
who departed this life
August 22 1825
aged 25 years

38.

Illegible

39.

Illegible

40.

Sacred
to the memory of
Catherine Coats
wife of
Sergeant William Coats
88th Regiment
Died 6 December 1829,
aged 28 years

41.

Sacred
to the memory of
Elisabeth, wife of George
Barrow, private soldier,
31 of King's Own Light Infantry
who died in childbirth 3 April 1831
in the 28 year of her age

42.

Sacred
to the memory of
Elizabeth Henriette Holder
daughter of William Holder
died 15 July 1835, 51 years of age

43.

Sacred
to the memory of
Adam Kellock, late
Barrack Sergeant, who departed
this life on the 3rd March 1847,
aged 53 years

44.

Illegible

45.

Illegible

46.

Illegible

47.

Illegible

48.

Captn J Scott

49.

Sacred
to the memory of
William Calvert
Soldier of the XI Regiment who
departed this life 27 July 1828
21 years of age

50.

Sacred
to the memory of
William Weale
Hospital Sergeant of the 90 Regiment
who departed this life 3 December
1830, aged 45 years

51.

Erected
by
Francis Watts
5 Regiment, to the memory of
his daughter who departed this life
on the 19th day of June 1836
aged 1 year and
10 months

52.

Sacred
to the memory of
Francis Lennox
Seaman of HMS *Aigle*
who died at Corfu 22 October 1842
aged 20 years
This stone was erected by his
Shipmates as a token of respect

53.

Here lie the remains of
Thomas Cope
Boy 1st Class
Belonging to HMS *Cyclops* & Born 1821
Died 14 August 1842, aged 20 years

54.

Sacred
to the memory of
James Barber,
Private 77th Regiment, who died
10th December 1842, aged 57 years
O Lord, whose mercy is so great,
Whose graces are confined,
Shall protect with protecting hand
The Babes I've left behind
Engraven deeply on their hearts.
This stone was erected by his comrade
of D Company as a token of respect

55.

Sacred
to
the memory of
Mary Ann Lee, wife
of Color Sergeant James Lee of the Royal
Artillery, who departed this life
on the 26 day of October 1827
aged 36 years

56.

Sacred
to the memory of
Sergeant J Gibbs
9 Regiment, who departed this life
23rd May 1841,
aged 42 years
This stone was erected by his comrade
Sergeants as a token of the respect
& esteem in which he was held by them

57.

Sacred
to the memory of
Mary, late wife of Thomas Jameson
97th Regiment, who departed this
life suddenly of apoplexy on the
17 July 1841, aged 24 years
Erected to the memory of
Josephine, aged 7 months
William, aged 5
Maria, aged 8
and Henry Percy Mackenzie, aged
4 years. 1853

58.

Henry Gibbons
aged 2 years
who died at sea, 29 Decr 1859
also
Lucy Eliza, born and died
10 August 1836

59.

Sacred
to the memory of
Doctor Benjamin Usher Hamilton
late Surgeon
16th Regiment of Foot
who departed this life 28 day of
March 1850, aged 34 years
His brother officers by whom he was
much beloved, as a token of respect
to his memory

Graduating from Glasgow University in 1837, Hamilton was an Assistant Surgeon from February 1839, and was appointed Surgeon in 1847.

60.

Sacred
to the memory of
Caroline Kircudbright Davis
Born 20th March 1829
Died 24 November 1849
Implore peace

61.

In memory of
Compton Sabine Browne
who died after three days illness
on the 2nd of March 1849 in the 7th year of his age
He was only son of the late Henry
Sabine Browne, Captain of HM's
85th Regiment, Light Infantry and
of Isabel, his wife

62.

Sacred
to the memory of
John Cross
late Hospital Steward, RA
who departed this life 23 October
1835, aged 52 years
This stone was erected by his
affectionate son as a tribute of
gratitude to his beloved father

63.

Sacred
to the memory of
Richard Pimlott
Company's Sergeant of the Royal
Artillery, who departed this life
at Corfu on the 3 January 1834
aged 32 years.
Also
to the memory of three of his infant
children, who are buried near this spot

64.

Sacred
to the memory of
Jane Smith, wife of Wm Smith
who died suddenly of apoplexy on the
27th June 1841,
aged 35 years

65.

Sacred
to the memory of
Jane, wife of Color Sergeant
William McLeod, Roy Sappers
& Miners, who departed this life
aged 43 years
Also two children, who died
in their infancy

66.

This stone was erected
by the crew
of HMS *Sapphire*
In testimony of their respect
for the memory of
John Watson
Late Armourer of the above ship who
suddenly called into eternity
by bursting a blood vessel on the
4th day of October 1836
aged 35 years
Jane McLeod, John Watson HMS *Sapphire*
C W Wray, HMS *Sapphire*, E Brown

67.

Sacred to the
memory of
Charles William Wray,
late musician
belonging to HMS *Sapphire*
who departed this life
December the 7th 1835
aged 35 years
This stone is voluntarily erected
as a token of respect
by the Petty Officers, Seamen &
Marines of the above ship

68.
Sacred
to the memory of
Edward Brown, private in the
9th Company of Royal Sappers & Miners
who departed this life on the
9th October 1830
aged 30 years
This stone was erected by his
Commander as a token of respect

69.
Sacred
to the memory of
Wm Wilson
late soldier, 12 Royal Highlanders
who departed this life on the
15th August 1855

70.
William Bastom
Born 1st March 1846
Died 26 June 1848

71.
Sacred
to the memory of
Richard Henry Hegett
who died at Corfu
September 18, 1848
aged 4 years

72.
Sacred
to the memory of
William Gregory
who departed this life
12 February 1855
aged 86 years

73.

Sacred
to the memory of
James Mitchell Cooper
son of
Sergeant Major I Cooper
who departed this life
11 of April 1850
aged 11 years

74.

Sacred
to the memory of
Clara Hurst, daughter of E P Hurst
Bandmaster of the 11 Light Infantry
who departed this life March 27, 1830
aged 7 years

75.

Sacred
to the memory of

2nd Corp William Taylor	15 June 1848	35½
Private John Eddiken	4 Sept 1848	32½
Private George Leader	5 Oct 1848	19½
2nd Corpl Robert Williams	22 Octr 1848	28½
Private George Herring	21 Febry 1849	30¼
4th Corpl James Odgers	17 July 1859	28
Private John Potter	7 Sept 1859	22
2nd Corpl James Harries	29 Dec 1859	28½
Private John McKilay	11 July 1859	29½

Late of the third Company of the
Corps
of
Royal Sappers & Miners

76.

Sacred
to the memory of
James Wadey
Private Solider 88 Regiment
who departed this life on the
30th day of July 1836
aged 39 years
This stone was erected by his affectionate
wife Mercy

77.

Sacred
to the memory
of James Tunnutt
Private, Royal Marines
of HMS *Vernon*
Died 2nd March 1842
aged 23 years
Beneath this stone Death's prisoner lies.
The stone shall move, the prisoner rise,
When Jesus with Almighty word,
Calls his dead Saints to meet their Lord
This stone was erected by his comrades
as a mark of their esteem & respect

78.

Sacred
to the memory of
James Cooke
Private, 77 Regt
who died 28 October 1842, aged 32 years
This stone was erected by his comrades
of D Company as a mark of their
regard and to show how sudden his
death took place, he having fell
dead when in the Ranks at a Brigade
Field Day

79.

Sacred
to the memory of
William Rudge
late Private Soldier
in Captain Wilson's Company
90th Light Infantry
Formerly in
the 58th Regt, who departed this
life on the 13th of September 1830
aged 38 years
This stone was erected by his brother
Soldiers as a testimony of their
esteem and regard

80.

Sacred
to the memory of
Thomas Cousins
Late Sergeant in the band of the
11 Regt of Foot who departed this
life on the 18th day of March 1831
aged 31 years

81.

Sacred
to the memory of
Sergeant William Bass
1st Battalion Rifle Brigade
who departed this life
August 22, 1843
aged 24 years

82.

Charles Wright, Royal Artillery
To the memory of his son Robert
who died September 14, 1840
aged 13 years

83.

Sacred
to the memory of
Thomas George
Late Color
Sergeant, 7 Battalion
Royal Artillery
He died on the 17 August 1830
after a few hours illness
aged 41 years
leaving a widow and four daughters
to deplore his loss.
He was a kind husband and father, a good soldier
and an upright man.
This stone was erected by his
fellow Sergeants as a mark
of high esteem
and regard

84.
Sacred
to the memory of
Henry William Boehmer
2nd Battn 60 Regt
who departed
this life on the
25 Feby 1840
aged 12 years & 4 months

85.
Sacred
to the memory of
William Shiell, Private
Royal Staff Corps
who departed
this life on the 28 January 1830
aged 27 years

86.
Sacred
to the memory of
Thomas Broughton
late Captain of the Port
who departed this life 8th January
1813, aged 68 years

87.
Sacred
to the memory of
Robert Fudler
Quarter Master HMS *Sybille*
died 25 August 1825
aged 49 years

88.
Sacred
to the memory of
Sergeant James Pearson
1st Battn Rifle brigade
who departed this life
October 5th AD 1843
aged 30 years

89.

Sacred
to the memory of
Hezekiah Budding
Royal Marines
of
Her Majesty's Ship *Actaeon*
Died 30 October 1831
aged 30 years

90.

Sacred
to the memory of
Thomas Phillip Newall
Infant son of Col Sergeant
Thomas Newall
and Ann Newall, his wife
King's Own Light Infantry
who departed this life 28
October 1832, aged 16 months

91.

Sacred
to the memory of
Thomas Fisher
Armorer Sergeant, 18 Royal
Irish Regiment, who departed
this life on the 25 February 1830
aged 42 years

92.

Sacred
to the memory of
Mark Coombs
aged 39 years
A native of Boston, Mass
Late Petty Officer on board the United
States Frigate *Potomac*
who departed this life
August AM 1836

93.
Sacred
to the memory of
P John McPherson of
the 42 Highlanders, who departed
this life on the 10 April 1836
aged 32 years
This stone is erected by his
comrades, soldiers of No 4 Company

94.
Sacred
to the memory of
David Ross
Private
Grenadier Company
77th Regiment
who departed this life 8th Sept 1842
aged 31 years

95.
Sacred
to the memory of
Henry Webber
late sergeant in the Royal Battalion
60 the King's Rifle Corps, who departed
this life on the 30 April 1837
aged 31 years

96.
Sacred
to the memory of
Charles Fanquier Esqre
who departed this life
on the 1st day of January 1848,
aged 50 years

97.
Sacred
to the memory of
Private George Heath
of the 55 regiment
who departed this life
on the 30 November 1856
aged 33 years

98.

Sacred
to the memory of
Oliver Walker, late Private
Soldier, 51 King's Own Infantry
who departed this life
the 19 October 1829
aged 37 years

99.

Sacred
to the memory of
Corinn Fanquier
who died 30 December 1857,
aged 16 years

100.

Sacred
to the memory of
William Herapaith
late musician, 28th Regiment
who departed this life on the 9th day
of May 1825, aged 27 years
He lived beloved and died lamented
by all who knew him

101.

Sacred
to the memory of
Moses Horne, son of James
and Margaret Horne
Master of 18th OR Royal Irish Band
who departed this life 15 December
1824, aged 3 years

102.

Sacred
to the memory of
Margaret, late wife of Barrack
Sergeant
Francis Campbell,
who died 15 August 1843
aged 49

103.
Sacred
to the memory of
H Robert Dudley Fairfoot
son of Robert Fairfoot, Quarter
Master, Royal Brigade
who departed this life
25 August 1832, aged 1 year

104.
Sacred
to the memory of
Jane Harvey, infant daughter
of William Harvey
Colr Sergeant 18th Regiment
and Anne, his wife
died 22 August 1831
aged 9 months

105.
Sacred
to the memory of
William Wilson, son of
Louisa and James Wilson,
who departed this life on the 28th
December 1829, aged 22 months
Also
Catherine, daughter of the above
who departed this life on the
3rd July 1833, aged 1 year
and
Margaret, daughter of the above
who departed this life on the
16 August 1835,
aged 3 months

106.

Sacred
to the memory of
Robert Reid,
Corporal and Pensioner, Royal
Artillery, who departed this life
13 December AD 1862
aged 72 years
Dispenser for many years in the
Surgery of the Royal Artillery, Corfu

107.

Sacred
to the memory of
Eliza Reid, daughter of Robert
Reid, late Corporal, and of his
wife, Ellen, who departed this life
on the 31 March 1840
aged 20 months
Also
To his beloved wife, Helen Reid,
who departed this life on the 14 August 1852,
aged 54 years

108.

Sacred
to the memory of
Elizabeth Campbell,
daughter of Sergeant Francis
and Margaret Campbell,
11th Regiment, who departed this life
the 20th December 1829
aged 6 years, 7 months

109.

Sacred
to the memory of
Isabella Foy
who departed
this life in the 5th August 1852, aged
1 year. Also Wm Henry Foy, who died the
20 August 1852, aged 2 years

110.
Sacred
to the memory of
Susan Ford Graham
who died 23 January 1845
aged 2 years & 2 months
Also
Margaret Harriet Graham
who died 5th August 1845
aged one month.

111.
Sacred
to the memory of
John Lewis Norman
who died 8 May 1824
aged 52
This stone is erected by an old friend
R Martin

112.
Erected
by Corpl Robert Wells
2nd Battn 60 Rifles, to the memory
of his daughter, who died in infancy
Also
her aunt, Elisabeth Walsh, who departed
this life 26 July 1840
aged 12 years, 8 months

113.
Sacred
to the memory of
William Rycroft, who died
16th May 1846
aged 31 years

114.
Edward Rycroft, died 23
June 1845, aged 11 months
W J Rycroft,
died 10 June 1843,
aged 10

115.
Sacred
to the memory
of
John Beal, who died 5 March 1840
aged 57 years
Mary Ann Beal, died 23 August 1860,
aged 70 years
John Beal, their son, died 29 July 1842,
aged 26 years

116.
Sacred
to the memory of
Sarah Claridge, wife of
Sergeant William Claridge, of the
1st Battn Rifle Brigade
who departed this life
28 January 1840
aged 30 years

Small cemetery adjoining previous one

1.
Sacred
to the memory of
Thomas Walter Gaskeath
Orderly Room Clerk
2 Batt, 2 Queen's Royal Regiment
who departed this life
on the 25 day of August 1859,
aged 30 years
This stone is erected by his affectionate
Mother

2.

Sacred
to the memory
of
the undermentioned men of the 71st Highland Light Infantry
who died during the service
of the Regiment in Corfu

Pte Wm Henderson　　Died 28 May 1853, aged 31
Sergt Wm McFarlane　　Died 19 Octr 1853, aged 29
Pte Jas Allan　　Died 23 Decr 1853, aged 19
Pte Rt Clark　　Died 15 Feby 1854, aged 35
Pte Jas Ross　　Died 25 Sepr 1854, aged 39
Pte Rt Baskett　　Died 26 Octr 1854, aged 33
Pte Jas Begbie　　Died 25 Novr 1854, aged 22
Pte Wm Stewart　　Died 7 Jany 1855, aged 33

Erected by the Non-Commissioned Officers &
Men of the Regiment

3.

Beneath this stone lies
in hope of resurrection to eternal
life and glory through his Lord and
Saviour, Jesus Christ,
Lewis Kekewich, Esquire
Lieut of HM's XX Regiment of Foot
Third son of Samuel Trehawke
Kekewich Esqre of Peamore in the
County of Devon
who died on the 16th February 1855
aged 18 years
He served in the Eastern Campaign
of 1854 with the British Army
and was present at the Battles of the
Alma, Inkerman and the Siege
of Sevastopol

Lewis Kekewich was born on 3 Sept 1836, the third son of Samuel Trehawke Kekewich, MP for Exeter 1826-30. He was commissioned Lieutenant in the 20th Regt of Foot and served at Alma, Balaclava, and was wounded at Inkerman. He died in Corfu. His older brother, Sir Arthur Kekewich was a member of the High Court of Justice.

4.

Sacred
to the memory of
Walter Montgomery Beresford
son of Captain G de la Poer Beresford
who died at Corfu, August 3rd 1853,
aged 9 months

George de la Poer Beresford (1826-1856) was the fifth son of Henry Beresford, the sixth son of Rt Hon John Beresford who was the younger brother of George, 1st Marquess Waterford (and also second son of Sir Marcus, 1st Earl of Tyrone). George, who served in Corfu was a Captain in the 16th Foot and married Annie, daughter of Lieut Gen Charles Conyers CB. They had three sons and one daughter, Walter being the youngest son. The oldest son, Charles, served as military attaché in St Petersburg.

5.

Sacred
to the memory of
Mary Sophia Harriet, the infant
daughter of Benhay and Mary
Elisabeth Martindale, Royal Engineers
Born 29th November 1849
Died 23rd October 1850

6.

Sacred
to the memory of
Mary Jane Anderson,
wife of James Anderson & Quarter
Master, 48 Regt, who departed this
life on the 21 May 1853
aged 1 year, 6 months. Likewise
two children, who died in their
infancy.
She was prepared to enter into that
which is reserved for the faithful in
Christ Jesus

7.

Sacred
to the memory of
Mary Jane Swaine
eldest daughter of Quarter Master
J Swaine, of the 2nd Battn Royal
Infantry, who died at Corfu 10 May 1855
aged 19 years

8.

Sacred
to the memory of
Susan Wise,
who died 16 August 1851
aged 60 years
She had been a faithful servant in
the family of the late General Ford,
Royal Engineers, for 10 years
and died in Corfu in the family
of Wm Walpole, his only surviving daughter
by whom this tablet is erected as a
tribute of respect to her virtues &
affection for her memory

9.

Eliza Fels
†
24 November 1851
John xiv 27, 28

10.

Entered into rest
24 July 1853
Helen
beloved wife of the Revd W Charteris
Presbyterian Minister, Corfu,
daughter of Reverend Paterson,
Wamphray, Dumfrieshire,
Scotland
A most affectionate wife and mother,
she died in faith, peace & hope.
Her last words were
"I hope to go to Jesus"

11.

Sacred
to the memory of
Thomas Greenwood
who departed this life 2nd of
December 1851, aged 45 years
This monument has been erected
by his beloved wife and son

12.

Erected
by Sergeants of the 2nd
Battn of the Royal Regiment
to the memory of the late
Color Sergeant H A Ferguson
of the said corps
who died 6 February 1854, aged 28 years
and left an affectionate wife to deplore her loss

13.

Sacred
to the memory of
Sapper William Shepherd
who departed this life 1st September 1856,
aged 20 years, 8 months
also
Sapper William Surcumbe, who died
15th September 1856
aged 20 years
This stone was erected by the NCO &
Sappers of the 9th Company R Engineers
as a tribute of Respect to their
departed comrade

14.

Sacred
to the memory of
Susan Amelia, the beloved daughter
of John and Emily West
who died on the 14th July 1859
aged 15 months

15.
Sacred to the memory of the
undermentioned
Gunner N Rickards, died Novr 7th 1855
Corpl E Harley, died 6 June 1857
Gr I Freeman, died 2nd Jany 1860
Gr W Fielding, died 17 Novr 1857
Gr J Wyard, died 9 August 1859
This stone is erected by the Non-C Officers
and Gunners of Lieut Colonel Honble E T Gage,
Company No 7, 18th Battn R Artillery
as a tribute of esteem to their departed
comrades

Edward Thomas Gage, the second son of the 4th Viscount Gage, was born in 1825 and commissioned in the Royal Artillery in 1844. A Brigade Major in the Crimean War, he died in 1889.

16.
Sacred
to the memory of
Eliza Hay,
only child of Captain Fattnald,
92 Highlanders, Born 10 February 1851
Died 19 October 1852

17.
Sacred
to the memory of
Edmund Gisbourne Peel,
3rd son of the Revd H P Wright,
Chaplain to the Forces, who died
Septr 22, 1852, aged 7 months

Henry Press Wright studied at Durham University and St Peter's College, Cambridge, becoming curate of Croscombe, Somerset 1841-43, and Frome-Selwood, also in Somerset 1843-44. He was then curate of Guiseley, Yorkshire 1844-45 and perpetual curate of St Mary, Leeds 1845-46. From 1846 to 1851 he was Chaplain to the Forces in Cephalonia and the Southern Ionian Islands, and from 1851 to 1854 was Chaplain in Corfu. During the Crimean War he served with the forces and after four years as archdeacon of British Columbia, he spent eleven years in Portsmouth as Chaplain to the Forces. Wright then returned to Canada as archdeacon of Vancouver Island and canon of Christ Church, Victoria 1876-80, before becoming rector at Greatham, near Petersfield from 1880 until his death in 1892. He wrote many books including *Recollections of a Crimean Chaplain*.

18.
>
> Sacred to the memory of
> Alice Telford,
> Infant daughter of William and Ellen
> Mackintosh, who departed this life
> 28 December 1859
> aged 13 months

19.
>
> Sacred to the memory of
> Henry Loftus Reade,
> aged 2 years and 8 months, the
> beloved son of Henry Cooper Reade
> and
> Elisabeth Reade,
> who departed this
> life March 13th, 1854, Corfu

20.
>
> To the memory of
> Rachel Eliza, the beloved daughter of
> George and Grace Jarvis,
> who died 10 Septr 1858, aged 12 months
> Also William & Henry, sons of above
> died 30 Octbr 1859, aged 10 months

21.
>
> Sacred
> to the memory of
> Henry Dores, late Blacksmith of
> HMS *Swallow*, who died 30 August
> 1857, aged 30 years

22.
>
> --
> youngest child of
> Captain J L Whitmore,
> Royal Engineers

23.
>
> To the memory of
> Joseph I B C Flack
> died 12 July 1855
> aged 40 years

24.
To the memory of
James Pollen
Seaman, HMS *Ariel*
who was drowned, Feby 18, 1858
in the 21 year of his age
This stone was erected by the Ship's Company
of HMS *Ariel*, as a token of respect to the
deceased.

25.
To the memory of
George Henry Ware,
son of Colr Sergt Charles Ware
L Company 91 Regiment, who died
at Corfu on the 4th March 1857,
aged 6 years, 4 months

26.
Joan Frances Collinson
Born in Corfu, Jany 3, 1858,
Died Jany 1859

27.
Ellen Rose Clark, born Novr 26, 1852
Died June 1856
"Be not afraid, only believe"

28.
Gilbert John Buchanan
Born 11 Septr, Died 21 December 1857

29.
To the memory of
Emma, the beloved child of William
& Jane Bowen] who departed this
life 30 July 1858, aged 1 year
"The Lord gave and the Lord hath taken away:
blessed be the name of the Lord."

30.
Edward G R Bowen
Born January 15 1857
Died January 27
"Suffer the little Children to come unto Me."

Edward George Roma Bowen was the oldest son of Sir George Ferguson Bowen (1821-1899) and his wife Comtessa Diamantina (née da Roma). Sir George was educated at Charterhouse and Trinity College, Oxford. He gained a 1st Class Degree in Classics and took up an appointment as Secretary of Government, Ionian Islands 1854-59. He was Governor of Queensland 1859-68, New Zealand 1868-73, Victoria 1873-79, Mauritius 1879-83, Hong Kong 1883-87 and then Royal Commissioner to Malta in 1888. The author of several books, his family tree was published in Hugh Gilchrist, *Australians and Greeks, Vol 1: The Early Years* (Rushcutters Bay, NSW 1992), p372-73.

31.
Arthur von Kruedener
Geb d XXIII Jany MDCCCLXVI
in Corfu
Gest XXI Juni MDCCCLXVI
Ev Merci, Cap x, xiv
Lasset die Kidlein
Zu mir kommen
und wehret ihnen nicht
Dem Solcher ist Das
Reich Gottea
Zur erinnerungen

32.
George Helmensdoffer
von Lindan
Entschlafen
den 14 Januar 1858
seinem treven mitarbeiter
das Hans Gels S, &c, C.

33.
Sacred
to the memory of
Mary Ann Elden,
wife of John Saruchi
born 8th June 1788
Died 5 July 1859

34.

Sacred
to the memory of
William Thomas Foster, who
departed this life 11th November 1855
aged 1 year & 6 months
also
Elizabeth Foster, who died 12 Novr 1855,
Aged 3 years & 8 months
Erected by their father
Robert Foster, Royal Artillery

35.

Ellen Woodman, the beloved
daughter of Corporal James & Eliza
Woodman, 16 Regt,
who departed this life 13th Septr 1858,
aged 11 months

36.

Sacred
to the memory of
..
the Royal Berkshire Militia,
who died at Corfu 1855
By the Officers of the Regiment

37.

Sacred
to the memory of
Sergeant Henry Organ, Royal Artillery
who departed this life on the 11th
Novr 1855, aged 27 years
This stone is erected by his Brother NC
Officers as a token of their esteem
for his gallant and exemplary
conduct while serving with the
British Army in Crimea

38.
Sacred
to the memory of
Thomas F R Marriott,
2nd son of Captn Marriott, 82 Regt, aged 15 months
Died 14 November 1855 at Corfu

39.
Sacred
to the memory of
Daniel Stratton Collings Esqre
late Captain 82 Regiment
who died on board the Transport
Bahiaria, at Malta on his passage
from England on the 30 January 1855
aged 27 years

40.
Laura,
the only daughter of
Colonel, the Honourable Berkeley Woodhouse,
Resident of Zante,
was born March 21, 1838
and died May 9, 1855
aged 17 years
"The Lord gave and the Lord hath taken away: blessed be the name of the Lord"

41.
Sacred
to the memory of the undermentioned men of the Grenadier Company
Royal Wiltshire Militia, who died on service at Corfu
Pte Thos Raisey, died 20 August 1855, aged 22 years
Pte James Maslin, was stabbed by an inhabitant
at the Esplanade when returning to
his Barracks at Tattoo on the 4th Septr
and died on the 5th Septr, aged 26 years
Sergt Thomas Connock, died 17 Octr 1855
aged 28 years, leaving an affectionate
widow to lament his loss

SANT ROCCO or NEW BRITISH CEMETERY

1.

To the memory of
William Cromer, Esqre LLD
of Mountjoy Square, Dublin
who died at Corfu on
the 15th of March
1878
aged 58 years
Erected by his beloved wife
Susanna S Crozier

2.

Sacred
to the memory of
James William Taylor
British Vice-Consul
who departed this life February
14th 1879, aged 59 years
Deeply regretted by his family & friends

3.

Sacred
to the memory of
Henry Thomas Gardiner,
eldest and beloved son of
George R & Mary Anne Gardiner
Born at Liverpool, England
June 1843
Died Corfu, June 15th 1863

4.

Sacred
to the memory of
Frances Matilda,
the beloved wife of
J C Powell
who died at Corfu
the 14th of January
1863, aged 26

5.
Sacred to the memory of
John William,
the son of James Parrot Arrowsmith
Quarter Master Battn 9th Regt
who departed this life at Gibraltar
on the 23 March 1831
aged one year & 3 months
Also of his daughter
Esther
who departed this life at Corfu
on the 22 June 1860
aged 11 months

6.
In memory of
William Dixon Esqre
Late
Captain, Royal Artillery
and for many years
Captain of the Port
of Corfu
who died on the 21 November
1859, aged 64
Also of his wife
Cecilia Peorina

7.
In loving memory of
Mathew John Page
Born 20th January 1820
Died 19 August 1870
Also Charlotte Page
Died 2 September 1897, aged 70

8.
Sacred
to the memory of
Carolina Antonia Aichinger
the beloved wife of
George Thomas Beal
who died 20th November 1876
RIP
Also of the aforesaid
Thomas George Beal
who died at Corfu 1892
aged 66 years

9.

Sacred
to the memory of
Captain R W Forrest
Late Commander
in the Ionian Government
Service
who departed this life
on the 1st December 1883,
aged 87 years
Also of his two sons
George, who died at Malta on the
18th Sept 1858, aged 26 years
James who died at Corfu on the 23
August 1854, aged 24 years

10.

To the memory of
Arthur Maxwell Earle,
Major, unattached, in Her
Majesty's Service,
Knight of the Legion of Honour
of France, and of Turkish Order
of the Medjidie
Born November 9th, 1832
Died March 9th, 1863.

11.

Sacred
to the memory of
Francis Goodrich, youngest
daughter of Deputy Commissr
General F B Archer, B: 14th
June 1857. D: 5th September
1860

12.

Sacred
to the memory of
Louisa Helen, the beloved
child of William Tharding,
Asst Surgeon, 1st Battn
25 Regiment, who
departed this life
October 9, 1860,
aged 14 months

13.
In memory of
Alice,
daughter of John Harley Esqre
Surgeon, 2nd Queen's Regt,
who died 21 February 1861,
aged 4 months

14.
Beneath this stone lie
the mortal remains of
Surgeon J Campbell

15.
Sacred
to the memory of
William Swann
who died 14th March 1879
aged 71
and of his wife
Hannah Maxwell Swann,
who died 11 February 1883
aged 94
RIP

16.
Sacred
to the memory of
William Swann,
who died at Port Said, Egypt
and of Edward Swann,
who died in Corfu
sons of
William and Hannah Swann

17.
In memory of
Wm McMahon MD
Assistant Surgeon, RN
who died at Corfu, 20 June 1871
aged 33
Erected by his brother officers
HMS *Prince Consort*

18.
In memory of
Ada,
infant daughter of Surgeon
Major Gay RA
and
Frances Mary,
his wife, 1863

19.
To the memory of
Major H A Vernon,
Royal Artillery
Died at Corfu, December 1862
aged 37

20.
Sacred
to the memory of
Joseph Thomas Carvill
of Newry, Ireland
who died at Corfu on the 3rd
May 1876
In the 26th year of his age

21.
To the memory of
Lieut Thomas Taylor
1st Battn, 9th Regiment
who died 4th September 1860,
aged 32

22.
SM
George William Gifford
Lieut, Royal Engineers
age 22 years
who was accidentally killed
while riding in the woods of
Corfu
on the 5th April 1864
This stone is erected by his brother
Officers

23.
MS
Gertrude Everin Page
Born July 14th, 1860
Died September 17th, 1874
Also Ina Annie Page
aged 8 months

24.
Sacred to the memory of
Esther, wife of William Kind
who departed this life
on the 17th May 1862,
aged 31 years

25.
Sacred
to the memory of
Thomas Fyers [Tyler?]
son of the late
William Fyers Esqre, 11th Foot
and grandson
of General Thomas Fyers
Royal Engineers
Born 28th December 1840
Died 28th December 1867

26.
In memory of
Lady Emily Cozziris
who died
March 23rd 1860

27.
Sacred
to the memory of
Captain the Honourable
Robert Le Poer Trench RN
Third son of Richard [2nd Earl Clancarty] GCB
Died at Corfu
April 19, 1867,
aged 57 years

Robert Le Poer Trench was born in Oct 1809, his father being Ambassador to The Hague from 1813 (he was created a peer of the United Kingdom as Viscount Trench in 1815, and Viscount Clancarty in 1818). Robert joined the Royal Navy and married, on 14 April 1847, Catherine Maria Thompson, daughter of John Thompson of Clonfin, co Longford, Ireland, and they had a son, Richard (1851-1907).

28.
To the memory of
Martha Flack, daughter of the late
Thomas and Martha Flack
died on the 14 of February 1868
aged 32

29.
Emma Louisa Ann
Born 7 March; died 20 August 1858
Infant daughter of
Revd William and Eliza Charteris

30.
30 April 1861
Departed in peace
Eliza
beloved wife of
Revd W Charteris
daughter of the late
W Lewis Esqre, Malta

31.
Sacred to the memory of
James Woodhouse,
a Companion of the Order of St Michael and St George
Formerly Deputy Commissionary
General in the British Army
and subsequently Treasurer
General of the Ionian States
under the British Protectorate
Died at Corfu on the 26 February
1866, aged 85

32.
Sacred
to the memory of
Abraham Carter
who departed this life
24 March 1862,
aged 78

33.
Sacred to the memory of
Jane Carter
who died 8th July 1872
aged 80 years

34.
Sacred to the memory
of
Edward J Blanckley,
Major, 6th Royal Regt
who departed this life
Novr 30th 1862
aged 46

35.
Sacred
to the memory of
John Thompson
who died January 30, 1879
aged 67 years
Also
to the memory of
Ann Longstaff,
Half-sister to the above
who died Jany 22, 1894, aged 78

36.
Sacred
to the memory of
Mary,
the beloved wife of
Mr Charles Hatton,
Chief Engineer in the
Ionian Government Service
who departed this life
9 August 1861
aged 50

37.
To the memory
of our
children Winifred Emma Isabella
and Bernard Cyrian Edward Bridge
1861
Erected by their parents
Captain, Royal Engineer
and Isabella, his wife

38.
Anne Osborne,
wife of Colonel George Winn
Commanding Royal Engineer
in the Ionian Islands
Died 29 May 1864,
aged 56 years

39.
Anny Elisabeth
eldest daughter and child
of Henry Drummond Wolf
and of Adeline, his wife
Born at Florence, October
20th, 1855
Died at Corfu, 23 Febr 1862

40.
The Revd
George Pigott Sutton MA
For six years
British Consular Chaplain
of Corfu
who died 5th July 1870
aged 35 years
Erected by several members
of the British Community

George Sutton was the third son of William Sutton of Brill, Bucks, gentleman. He attended Magdalen Hall, Oxford, matriculating in Nov 1853. He graduated BA and MA in 1862.

41.
In memory of
Sir Charles Sebright KCMG
Baron d'Everston
who died at Corfu
9 October 1884
also of Georgina Mary
Lady Sebright,
Baroness d'Everton
who died at Corfu
24 January 1874

Sir Charles Sebright married Georgina Mary, daughter of Sir William Pitt Muir Mackenzie, 2nd Bart, 24 Nov 1871. She wrote, with Adelaide Irby, *Travels in the Slavonic Provinces of Turkey in Europe* (London 1866).

42.
Sacred to the memory of
Charles Robert
who departed this life
the 10th Sept 1862, aged 9 months
only and beloved son
of Colonel Elenhurst
10th Regt, and his wife
Frances [Elderhost?]

43.
Sacred
to the memory of
James Frances
the beloved son of
Lt Colonel Robertson
Deputy Quarter Master General
in the Ionian Islands
and Heston Matilda, his wife
who died at Corfu
on the 20 March 1863
After a few hours' illness
aged 3½ years

44.

Sacred
to the memory of
Mercy Knocker
widow of Thomas Knocker Esqre
and daughter of the late
Sir John Hollams
Both of Kent
who departed this life
on the
8th September 1874,
aged 79
Also of
Henry Leopold Elic Elefebure
(Grandson of the above)
Born at Liverpool, 4th Sept 1840
Died at Corfu
2 January 1897

45.

In memory of
Ernest Trest
infant son of G E Gains
Surgeon, 6 Royal Regt
Died 28 October 1863

46.

---
child
of
W J E Newton
11 January 1863

47.

Sacred
to the memory of
John de Norman
Died Decr 18, 1868
Sacred
to the memory of
Emma de Norman
Died October 5, 1876
within 2 days of her 20 years

48.
Gladys Zoe Carlisle
daughter of the Revd
J W Conway Hughes, MA
HBM Chaplain at Corfu
Died Sept 16, 1878
aged 2 years and 6 months

Rev John William Conway Hughes was the eldest son of John William Hughes of Holywell, Oxford. He was educated at Trinity College, Oxford, matriculating in May 1842, aged 18. He was a scholar at Corpus Christi College 1842-45 and New Inn Hall, gaining his BA in 1849 and MA in 1851. Hughes was Consular Chaplain at Corfu 1870-82.

49.
In loving memory
of
Edward Frederick Barr
who died 27 Novr 1881
aged 72

50.
In loving memory of
James Quinland
died April
1887
aged 52 years

51.
In memory of
John Woodley
who died at Corfu
May 9, 1887, aged 78
Also of
Sophia Lissa,
his wife, who died at Zante
15 October 1880
Erected by their son
Thomas John Woodley

52.
In loving memory of
John Stretch
Born at Liverpool
Died at Corfu
October 9, 1889, aged 84

53.
Sacred
to the memory of
Olin Bardenfletch
née Sanshot
B: Denmark 1849;   D: Corfu
1888

54.
In loving memory of
Catherine Johnston
widow of the late
Robert Johnston
of Cashel
in the Coy Donegal, Ireland
who died at Corfu July 24, 1884
aged 68 years

55.
In loving memory of
Countess Penelope Valsamari
Born 8 February 1831
Died March 1887

56.
Mrs Prascodima

57.
In honoured and ever loving
memory of
Fred C Brown
for many years HBM Vice Consul
for Ibraila, Roumania
who departed this life at Corfu
January 10, 1888, aged 67
His daughters, Elizabeth, Emily, Edith,
RIP

58.
In every loving memory
of my beloved husband
Frederick Murphy
late British Vice Consul
for Ibralia, Roumania
who departed this life
at the age of 51, Corfu, Novr 1895

59.
In affectionate memory of
Thomas Grant
of
Bhangulpore, Bengal
who died at Corfu
on the 29 March 1890,
aged 64 years

60.
Sacred to the memory
of the
Revd Ernest Lytton MA
who died at Corfu
(after a short illness)
This monument is erected by the
community in affectionate remembrance
of their late pastor and friend

61.
In loving memory of
Ellen Victoria Barry
the beloved wife of
George Raymond, Superintendent
Eastern Telegraph Company
who died at Corfu
June 23rd 1892

62.
Mrs Manetta

63.
Thomas J Woodley

II

1.
Sacred to the memory of
Elisabeth Margaret
the beloved daughter of
M & M Downey
2nd Battn, 9th Regiment
who departed this life
on the 19th April 1863
aged 6 months & 4 days

2.
Sacred to the memory
of
Mary Hannah Jane
the beloved daughter
of
M & T Henry
.. Battn, 9 Regiment
who departed this life
on the 1 March 1863
age 1 year, 1 month

3.
> Gustav Spenglin
> geb 8 Novr 1868
> gest 18 Nov 1868

4.
> Elwina Spenglin
> geb 19 April 1873
> gest 3 April 1874

5.
> Oswald Fels
> 16-19 Januar
> 1880

6.
> In memory of
> William Christian-Deverell
> Late Captain of the Port of
> Corfu
> who died 9 July 1878
> aged 62 years

7.
> James Jameson, aged 78 years
> died 29 Decr 1879

8.
> Eliza Mackenzie, aged 75 years; died 14 Feby 1881

9.
> Frederick Gysi
> [Swiss]
> died 1 April 1882, aged 77 years

10.
> Rubt in Trieden
> Gertrude Spenglin
> geb Hirschfeld ans Chevensick
> geb 25 Februar 1837
> gest 25 Januar 1885

11.
>
> Dem amdenken au
> Jakob Wartman
> geb Imdan; d 2 Oct 1856
> gest Corfu 26 Juni 1889

12.
>
> Hier Ruket in Gott
> Bertha Fels
> G Spenglin

13.
>
> Qui reposa
> Antonio de Cornory
> Secretario Aulieve Ministeriale
> presso l'TER Ministero
> affari esteri
> A Vienna
> Nato li 2 Febrajo 1852
> Morte at Corfu li 7 Aprile 1889
> Dopo lunga e pemosa Malattia

14.
>
> Alexius Folvery

15.
>
> Elwina Heimpel
> geb 10 Oct 1888
> gest 23 August 1892
> Es war ein sonnenschen

16. [No monument erected.]
> Thomas Fels, died 19 Novemr, aged 40 years

17. [No monument erected.]
> Martin Fels, died 3 July, aged 81 years

18.
>
> Robert Heimpel, Dutch Consul; born 20th Sept
> 1855; died 9 February 1897
> Pelichtiren und del warest du

III

1.
To the following Non-Commissioned Officers and privates of the 1st Battn, 9th Regt, who died during their service in the Ionian Islands from 1859 to 1864:

Corpl J Thomas	Corpl M Donolan
Pte T M Cure	Pte J Satchfield
Pte J Burke	Pte J Shankey
Pte M Butler	Pte R Longstands
Pte B Williams	Pte G Green
Pte J McElligot	Pte J Donolan
Pte T Landstaff	Pte J Williamson
Pte W Parker	Pte W Gould
Pte S Watson	Pte J Ganderton
Pte H Evans	Pte J Hillier
Pte C Cook	Pte J Homer
Pte W Crump	Pte J Barnett
Pte M Curtain	Pte J Coaggs
Pte W Dowling	Pte M Roach

2.

S to M
of Sarah Wentworth
3rd daughter of W C Wentworth Esqre
of Vaucluse, Sydney, Australia
Born August 1st 1835
died Decr 23, 1857
The remains of the above named were
removed from the British Cemetery to
Sydney, N S Wales, 1872

William Wentworth was born in 1790, his mother being Catherine Crowley, a convict being transported to Norfolk Island and the father D'Arcy Wentworth being the medical officer on the same boat – who acknowledged paternity. William Wentworth went on to become an explorer, author, barrister, landowner and statesman. He died in 1872.

3.

Erected in memory of

Pte John Fix	Pte William Leech
Pte John Hucker	Pte James Roster
Pte Charles Mayne	Pte John E Cox
Pte John Blaker	Pte John Elect
Pte William Brown	Pte William Lyons

Serjt Edwin Gruby
Died 1859

Pte William Came   Pte Dennis Shipton

Died 1859

Pte John Smith	Pte John Browess
Pte John Petters	Pte Albert S Ray
Pte John Williams	Pte Joseph Bysooth
Pte James Mahaffey	Pte James Graham
Pte Richard Jones	L-Serjt John Brown

Died 1861

By their comrades of the 2nd Battn
4th of the King's Own Regt –

Sergt Thomas Perry	Sergt Adam Mitchell
Pte Joseph Maces	Sergt Thomas Bowyer
Pte Thomas Savage	Pte William Watkins

Died 1863

4.

Sacred
to the memory of
the Non-Commissioned Officers and Sappers of the
29th & 30th Companies, Royal Engineers
who died during their service at Corfu

29th Company
Sergt E Ciles, died 3rd August 1859
aged 33 years
Sapper N Davies, died 31 Jany 1861
aged 30 years
Sergt C Seall, died 16th Jany 1864
aged 35 years

III

1.
80th Company
Sapper Trussell, died 16th Sept^{er} 1861,
aged 24 years
Serjt Jenkins, died 18th October 1861,
aged 32 years
Sapper C Horton, died 29 Sept 1862,
aged 24 years
Corpl J Frost, died 6th Novr 1863,
aged 35 years
Lc-Corpl R Wood, died 17th April 1864,
aged 26 years
Erected by the N-C Officers and
sappers of the 29th and 30th Companies
as a mark of respect to their departed comrades

2.
Sacred to the memory of
Mary Catherine, the beloved daughter
of P & M C Boylan, 2nd Battn, 9th
Regt, who departed this life on the
3rd March 1860, aged 3 years &
6 months
Also
their son Patrick William,
who departed this life on the
30 June 1863,
aged 5 years & 3 days

3.
Sacred to the memory of
the beloved children of O R Mc
Sergt T Tully, 2nd Battn, 4th K O Regt
and Mary Ann, his wife, who departed [this life]
at Corfu as follows:

		Years	Months
John Michael	14/11/59	2	3
Thomas	27/4/63	4	0
Mich Fred	20/5/63	2	3

Also their cousin, Thomas Casey
10/5/63, years 2, months 5.

4.

Sacred
to the memory of
Mary Ellen Edith,
only child of Sergt C & E H Simpson
2nd Battn, 4th King's Own Regt
who died 14 October 1859,
aged 12 months

5.

Sacred
to the memory of
Richard Quigley Jones,
who departed this life on the 3rd July 1881, aged 17 years and 1 month
The above mentioned son of
Gr Sergt R C Jones, Rt Ers.

6.

Sacred
to the memory of
Harry Arthur, son of Schoolmaster
MacArley and his wife Emma,
the beloved child departed this life
on the 18th August 1862, aged 1 year
and 4 months
Also William MacArley,
who departed this life 13 February
1862, aged 3 years and 6 months

7.

Sacred
to the memory of
Martha Caroline, the third beloved
daughter of F C & J Swaffield
2/4th Regt, who departed this life
August 11, 1860, aged 16 months
Also Alex Swaffield
who departed
this life on the 10th July 1863
aged 13 months

8.

Sacred
to the memory of
Alice Caroline Page
daughter of Fredk William and
Frances Page, Purveying
Department, departed this life
5 October 1860,
aged 18 months

9.

Sacred
to the memory of
Charles Lockwood
the beloved son of Serjt J Lockwood
who departed this life on the 16th November 1860
aged 1 year and 8 months

10.

Sacred
to the memory of
Martha Elizabeth Westacott
who departed this life on the 10th
Sept 1861, aged 6 months
The above mentioned was the
beloved daughter of Sergt M & M A Westacott
In memory of Annie Westacott
who departed this life on the 11 Decr 1862
aged 2 months

11.

Alaric Barker

12.

Alexander Zillatoff Williontan

IV

1.

Sacred
to the memory of
William Bishop, Gunner of the
Royal Marines Artillery
who departed this life on the 21 of
May 1860 at Corfu

2.

In memory
of Richard F Lowdes
Staff Sergt Major, died 20th May 1860
aged 43

3.

Sacred to the memory of
Joseph Dawson Edwards
late ordinary Seaman of HMS *Liffey*
who was killed falling
from the toretor May 10, 1800,
aged 21 years

4.

Sacred
to the memory of
William D Epwartby,
a man belonging to HMS *Caesar*
who departed this life Jany 1861
aged 21 years

5.

Sacred
to the memory of
Nicholas Brewer of HMS *St Jean d'Acre*
who departed this life on the 1st
of January 1850,
aged 22 years

6.

Sacred
to the memory of the undermentioned
private soldiers, HM 2nd Battn, 2nd
Queen's Royal Regiment,
who died at Corfu from typhus fever
Private W James, died 2nd August 1861
aged 23 years
Private W East, died 6th August 1861
aged 20 years
Privare John Sandelis, died 17th August 18--
aged 24 years

7.

Erected to the memory
of Robert Putton, Seaman, HMS
Marlborough, who departed this life
on the 25th November 1860,
aged 24 years

8.

Sacred
to the memory of
Franck Stapleton of HMS *[St] Jean d'Acre*
who departed this life on the 2 December
1859, aged 43 years. He was highly esteemed
by his shipmates, by whom this stone was erected.

9.

Sacred
to the memory of
Charles Young
late Pte, Royal Marine Lt Inf
who died 23rd October 1866,
aged 24 years

10.
To the memory of
William Smith,
leading seaman, gunner and diver
aged 24 years, who departed this life
28 Sept 1860 from the effects of apoplexy
brought on by over exertion while diving
for the recovery of two guns just in
the harbour
This stone is erected by the
Captain, Officers and Company of
HMS *Melpomene* as a mark of
their regard and testimony
of his worth

11.
Sacred
to the memory of
Mary Elisabeth, the beloved
and devoted wife of Color Sergt
James Elliott, 2nd Battn, 9th Regt
who departed this life on the
4 November 1859,
aged 22 years

12.
Sacred
to the memory of
Esaw Abbott, of HMS
St Jean d'Acre, who departed
this life on the 16 of November 1859,
aged 19 years

13.
Sacred
to the memory of
Thomas Fuller, Seaman of HMS *Hannibal*
who was killed by a fall from
aloft on board that Ship at
Corfu on the 22 of November 1859
aged 19 years

14. [Iron Cross]
John Peters
Pvt 4 Regt

15.

Sacred
to the memory of
Ellen, the beloved wife of
Pte W Byrom, 2st Bn, 9th Regt
who died 24 of March 1861
aged 27 years

16.

Sacred
to the memory of
Francis Gander, 1st Class boy,
HMS *Algiers*,
who departed this life 12 April 1861
aged 17 years and 7 months

17.

Erected by No 8 Battery
3rd Brigade RA as a token
of respect to their departed
comrades Gunner Geo Shilitoe,
who died at Corfu
on the 29th Sept 1861
Gunner Ed Ryan, killed
by an explosion of a gun at Vido
17 May 1863
Gunner Dd Griffin
died at Corfu, 11 September
1863

18.

Sacred
to the memory of
Ellen B Jackson of
Burton, was accidentally drowned
while bathing in the sea at Corfu
October 1861, aged 19 years

19.
Erected by No IV, Co 1st
Regt as a token of respect
to their departed comrade
Pte J Barnett
who died at Corfu VI October MDCCCLXI

20.
Here lies the mortal remains
of Henry Day
Private, Royal Marines Light
Infantry, who departed this life
on board HMS *Scylla*
16 November 1861
This tablet is erected by the marines
of the detachment in memory of
their departed comrade

21.
Sacred to the memory of
Faith Rennie, the beloved wife of Sergt
O Rennie, who departed this life on
the 17 January 1862, aged 46 years

22.
Sacred
to the memory of
Duncan McFarlane,
Seaman of HMS *Victor Emmanuel*
who departed this life on the
14th February 1862
aged 45 years

23.
Sacred
to the memory of
Fanny,
the beloved wife of E Shillington
RE, who departed
this life 17th May 1863
aged 28 years
Erected by her husband as a token
of love to a faithful wife and loving
mother

24.

Sacred
to the memory of
Alfred Wickendem
who was born 25 July 1836
Died July 29th 1862
He fell from aloft in the execution
of his duty
This tablet is erected as a token
of respect by his messmates and
topmates of HMS *Marlborough*

25.

James Miller
AB, HMS Queen
aged 23, died 1st September 1861

26.

Sacred
to the memory of
the late Sergt Chas Moore,
RMLI
HMS *Algiers*

27.

Frederick Dabourn
Second Wardroom, Steward
HMS *Algiers*,
died 31 August 1862,
aged 23 years

8.

Sacred
to the memory of
the beloved children of
Color Sergt Danby and Elisabeth
his wife, 2nd Battn 4th KO Regt
Emma, died 15th June 1863
aged 2 years, 5 months
Ellen, died 23rd June 1863
aged 8 months

29.

Sacred
to the memory of
Oswald Spencer
who died at Corfu on the
9th of December 1863
aged 5 years and 7 months
the beloved son of Staff
Sergt R Jeffery and his wife
Eliza

30.

Sacred
to the memory of
Caroline Steatham
who died at Corfu on the
10th February 1864,
aged 40 years

31.

Sacred
to the memory of
Sergt Thomas RA,
who died at Corfu on the 9th
February 1864, aged 34 years & 4 months

32.

Sacred
to the memory of
William Collings, Captain's
Coxswain of HMS *Surprise*
who departed this life
on the 4th January 1864,
aged 34 years

33.
To the following men of the
2nd Battn, 4th KO Regt
Pte John Fox, 1859
Pte William Lyons, who was killed
by a shark 7th August 1859
Pte John Peters, Pte John Williams, who
died in 1861
Pte William Watkins,
died in 1863
Erected by No 10 Company, 2nd Battn
4th KO Regt as a token of respect to
their departed comrades

34.
Sacred
to the memory of
Pte Rd Clarke
2nd Battn, 6th Regiment
who died 6th October 1862
aged 40 years
for 17 years faithful servant of
Major H R Cove, who erected this stone

35.
Sacred
to the memory of
Isabella,
the beloved wife of J Miall,
who departed this life on the
20th September 1863, aged 23 years
Also of his son
Charles William, who departed this life
On the 15th October 1863,
aged 1 year & 6 months

36.
Sacred
to the memory of
Esther, the beloved wife of
Joseph Graham
Warder, Military Prison, Vido,
who departed this life 3rd October
1863, aged 24 years

37.

Sacred
to the memory of
Wm Tarring,
Seaman of HMS *Orlando*
who departed this life the
6th October 1863,
aged 20 years
This stone was erected by his
Mess and Topmates

38.

Sacred
to the memory of
John Anderson, Serjt Major Commissariat
Staff Corps, who departed this life
at Corfu on the 14th Octbr 1863,
aged 26 years
& 11 months
Erected by the Officers of the
Comm Officers & Civil members
of the Commiss
and the Non-Comm Officers of the Staff

39.

Sacred
to the memory of
Robert Reid
Ordy Seaman of HMS *Phoebe*
who died in Corfu Roads on HMS
Terrible, Decr 29, 1865, aged 20 years
He was a native of Plymouth, England
This stone is erected by the Officers
& Ship Company of HMS *Terrible* as
a parting tribute of respect

40.
Sacred
to the memory of
Thomas Durban,
Chief Mate and Instructor of
HMS *Hydra*
who was accidentally shot
whilst in the execution of his duty
at Rifle practice 10 May 1864
aged 24 years & 7 months
This stone is erected by the Officers, Seaman & Marines as a mark of esteem
He was beloved by all who knew him

41.
Sacred
to the memory of
William Weale
who departed this life on the
10 March 1869,
aged 58 years
Erected by the wife as a token of love
to a faithful husband and loving Father

42.
Sacred
to the memory of
William Ward,
a native of Tollesbury, Essex
Seaman on Board the Yacht *Gellert*
who died in the Civil Hospital
of Corfu on the 29th day of December
1872, aged 27 years

43.
Hier Ruht in Gott
Babette Hoffman
aus Carlsruhe in Baden
Offeb Johannis 14, 13
Geb 23 April 1825
Zu Ichënan
bei Heidelberg
Gest 24 of August1874
aut der Ruchfreise
von Jerusalem
Naachder Heimath
Gewdimet von verwandten

44.

Sacred
to the memory of
Richard Weale
formerly HBM Vice-Consul
at Prevesa
Died August 2nd 1875
aged 56 years

45.

In memory of
James Hatherly
Ship's Cook of
HMS *Devastation*
who died in Corfu Oct 16th 1875,
aged 32 years

46.

Sacred
to the memory of
Ellen Elisabeth
Only beloved child of
Sergt Thos Seahan,
2nd Battn, 4th K O Regiment
and his wife Caroline
who departed this life
on the 13th June 1863,
aged 8 years & 6 months

47.

Alexander Corvin [German]
K R Rittmeister AD Starb 41 Jahre alt 19 May 1876

48.

Hier Rust
Babette Gaertner
Geb den 26 September 1860
Auf dem wege
Nach der Heimath
won tade crailt
Gest den 5 September 1876

49.
Hier ruhen in Gott
Unsere lieben Kinder
Amalis
Geb 12 August 1867
Gest 7 Septr
1867

50.
Otto Geb 4 Octr 1868; Gest 12 June 1869
Richard
Geb 4 April 1873; Gest August 1876
Johanna Magdalena
Geb 1 June 1871; Gest 15 August 1876
Wilhelm
Geb 31 Januar 1875; Gest 16 August 1876
die franernden eltern
Johannes & Amalie Frey

51.
Ernest Frey
Geb 26 April 1877
Gest 7 June 1879
Ruht Sanct

52.
Hier ruht in Gott
G R Emil Kloctzscker
Geb 6 July 1863
Gest 19 October 1866
Fried Peiner Asche

53.
In memory of
William & Catherine Frost
of the Royal Engineers
Catherine died 9th July 1863
aged 20 years
Her husband followed
November 1863,
aged 35 years
Also Georgina, their child, who died
6 January 1863

54.
All the little children of the
29 & 30 C RE
who died at Corfu

55.

Sacred
to the memory of
Edith Maud Whitfield
Born 10th August 1866
Died
27 August 1868

56.

Sacred
to the memory of
Marianne Helen Wilkin
Born 21st November 1868
Died 10th October 1869
and of
Ann Charlotte Wilkin
Born 14th August 1870
Died 4 June 1871
Also in memory of
Emily
wife of John Wilkin
who died in Corfu 13 October 1886
aged 44 years

57.

Sacred
to the memory of
Thomas Williams
of HMS *Iris*
Private RMLI
A native of Dowlais, South Wales
who died in Corfu
on the 28th of January 1881
aged 25 years
Erected by the Officers and
Marines of the Iris in token of their
esteem and regard

58.
Sacred
to the memory of
James Jenkins, Ship Steward
HMS *Cruiser*
who died at sea off Corfu
on Sunday – 1880,
aged 28 years
Erected by his shipmates
& friends in token of their esteem
& regard

59.
Joseph Phillips Incaman
B Schooner *Doris*

60.
Edward Thunder, Seaman
SS *Falerinian* (drowned)

61.
Sacred
to the memory of
my beloved husband
Francis Ershire Harvey
aged 37
a native of Greenock
who died on board SS *Saragossa*

62.
In memory of
Edgar Cramp
Ordinary Seaman of
HMS *Hecla*
who died 28 November 1887
aged 20 years
This stone was erected by his shipmates
as a token of respect

63.

Sacred
to the memory of
Thomas Smith
Seaman of HMS *Cruiser*
Died at Corfu 31 December 1887
aged 18 years
This stone was erected by his shipmates
in loving memory to him

64.

In remembrance of
William German
Gunner RMA, HMS *Thunderer*
died 12th August 1885,
aged 25 years
Erected to his comrades as a mark
of their esteem

65.

Sacred
to the memory of
Arthur Spittle
Able Seaman of HMS *Temeraire*
who died in Corfu of dysentery contracted
whilst serving with the Naval Brigade
during the war in Egypt
October 19th 1882, aged 21 years

66.

Robert Charlton, HMS *Temeraire*

67.

Sacred
to the memory of
William E Penny,
Signalman, HMS *Polyphemus*
Drowned at Corfu, 18th April 1887,
aged 24 years

68.

Charles Marshall, HMS *Edinburgh*

69.
Julia Papaviero

70.
Hier ruht in Gott der
Oberkeizer Alfred Menzel
von Board
SMS *Frederick der Grosse*, Geb 3 November 1870
Gest 10 Dezember 1889
Eum audenken errichtet von der
Besatzung SMS *Frederick der Grosse*

71.
Hier Ruht der Ober
Maschinist der Kaiserlick deutschen
Maciue Jean Ludeman
Geb den 7ten Marz 185-
Gestden 15th Februar 1891
Kameraden

72.
Heddel Leflufy,
Syrian (Protestant)

73.
George Worsley
Died 4 February 1894,
aged 68

74.
John Dyz, HMS *Ramillies*

75.
Edward Charles Jones, HMS *Cruiser*

76.
Edward Niel, stoker, HMS *Ramillies*

77.

Sacred
to the memory of
Corporal Michael Donnellan [or Dermottan?]
of the
1st Battalion, 2nd Regiment
aged 26 years
who was murdered by Private Joseph Chadwick
on the 28th day of October 1861

78.

Erected
to the memory of
P Patrick Shilton
who departed this life
10 August 1860, aged 21 years

79.

From earthly troubles and storms
Mary Graham, aged 26 years
has flown on the 10 March 1860
to eternal rest and happiness

80.

Sacred
to the memory of
Ellen Earnshaw, the beloved wife
of J Earnshaw, Band, 1st Battalion
9th Regiment, who departed this life
27th September 1862
aged 31 years
also
his son, James Earnshaw
who died 21 September 1862
aged 3 years and 1 month

81.

Sacred
to the memory of
Private John Hanly
No 10 Company, 2 Battn, 9th Regiment
who departed this life
on the 28th September 1862
aged 22 years

82.

Sacred
to the memory of
Catherine,
wife of Serjeant Major John Vince,
2nd Battalion, 9th Regiment
who departed this life
on the 25 February 1864
aged 30 years
also
George, son of the above
who died on the 7th February 1860
aged 8 months

83.

Sacred
to the memory of
the undermentioned Non-Commissioned
Officers & Men of the 2nd Battn, 9th Regt
who died in the Ionian Islands
between the 12th November 1838
and 21 May 1864

Color St O'Callanghan	Color St Gile
Serjt T Brogden	L Sert T Roche
Corl G Crowther	Corl H Hand
Corl M Hegarty	Corl D Stanyard
Private G Arter	Private R Hudson
Private J Ball	Private J Kempe
Private W Brogden	Private L Lingard
Private W Burns	Private J Mitchell
Private J Burton	Private J Mangan
Private C Clements	Private M Moran
Private J Connolly	Private J Pixton
Private R Cooper	Private P Seelton
Private H Elmer	Private T Shea
Private J Foster	Private S Soar
Private T Gibson	Private W Stanckyard
Private J Henley	Private E Trisley
Private J Bavill	Private H Webby
Private D Hogan	Private W Hight
Private J Kennedy	Private J Wyatt

Erected by the Non-Commissioned
Officers & Men of the 2nd Battn, 9th Regt
as a mark of their esteem for
their departed comrades

84.
Qui giace nella pace
dei guisti
Maddalena Burns (nata Wolf)
di Corfu
Mortchel eta di anni 32 il 15 Junio 1869
Il figlio Roberto Antonio
dolente pose

85.
Henry Stewart
Quarter Master, RN
HMS *Cruiser*
Died 18 June 1878,
aged 62 years
Erected by his shipmates

86.
Eleonor Deverell (lunatic)
wife of Wm Deverell

87.
Sacred
to the memory of
Robert Charlton,
Seaman of HMS *Temeraire*
who was killed by falling
from aloft at Corfu
aged 20 years
Erected by his shipmates

88.
Sacred
to the memory of
Patrick John Darral
writer, HMS *Dolphin*
who departed this life
7th August 1885,
aged 25 years

89.
                      Robert Blakaney
                  who departed this life
                       9th April 1886
                        aged 56 years
                             RIP

90.
                       Catherine Bass

91.
                        William Bass

92.
                   Frederick von Wimmar
                    Lieutenant zue see
               Maj Panzerschiff Preussen
                Geboren 14 Marz 1861
           Gestorben Am 12 Dezember 1889

[And another forty without tombstones.]

PROTESTANT CEMETERY, PAXOS

1.

Sacred
to the memory of
Major Henry Vernon of the
36 Regiment, who died
on the 2 June 1822

Henry Vernon was appointed Major on 25 Aug 1804.

2.

Sacred
to the memory of
Robert Blakeney
Captain of the 36 Regiment

3.

Sacred
to the memory of
I J Wm Maskell
late of the Royal Buffs, who
departed this life on the 26
December 1856

4.

Thomas Pace
who departed this life
on the 12 September 1845

5.

Frederick Dickens
who died on the 21 June 1848

6.

Alfred Stevens
who died on the 4th October 1855

ROMAN CATHOLIC CEMETERY, PAXOS

1.
              Lieut I F Wilkinson
           died 2 September 1820

2.
                Pvt Wm Boyle
             died 28 April 1852

3.
                John Scanlon
          died 27 August 1831

4.
                Arthur Brown
      who died on the 5th November
                    1854

Four tombs with inscriptions defaced

PROTESTANT CEMETERY, SANTA MAURA (LEVKAS)

There were 100 graves altogether, of which only a few had inscriptions surviving.

1.
Sacred
to the memory of
John Berridge
Gunner, 7 Batt
Royal Artillery
who departed this life on the 20 of
August 1834, aged 29 years

2.
Sacred
to the memory of
Gunner William George Meadows
who departed this life on the 3rd Novr
1814, aged 21 years

3.
Sacred
to the memory of
Gunner Joseph Morrison, 7 Battn
Royal Artillery, who departed this
life the 20 October 1833, aged 21 years

4.
Sacred
to the memory of
Stephen Edmonds Harpwood,
aged 24 years

5.
Sacred
to the memory of
William Tyers, Esqre, formerly of the
11 Regiment, Collector of Customs
at Santa Maura, who died suddenly on
the 29 December 1852 from heart disease,
aged 46 years

Santa Maura (Levkas): Roman Catholic Cemetery

6.
Sacred
to the memory of
Private Andrew Wm Moore
who departed this life on the 23 January
1833, aged 28 years

7.
Sacred
to the memory of
Gunner Daniel Buckley, 11th Battalion
Royal Artillery, who departed this life
on the 11 January 1832, aged 25 years

8. [White marble monument]
Sacred
to the memory of
Anne, the wife of Lieut Colonel
Keightlay, HM's XI Regiment of Foot
Resident of Santa Maura who
departed this life on November
6th 1831, aged 37 years

9. [Rose colour marble monument]
Richard C Lloyd, Esquire, late Ensign
in HM's 11 Battalion, who died at Santa
Maura on the 3 July 1848, aged 20
years

10.
Sacred
to the memory of
Color Sergeant George Burns, HBM's 97 Regiment
of Foot, who died at Santa Maura on the 10th
day of July 1841, aged 37

11.

Sacred
to the memory of
Jane Gilchrist
wife
of Corp James Gilchrist
2nd Battn,
Royal Regt of Artillery, who departed
this life on the 17 August 1862

12.

Ensign G Doyly, 10 Regiment, who died
at Santa Maura on the 7th day of August
1837, aged 20 years
This stone is erected by the Officers of his Regiment
in token of their esteem and regard

13.

Sacred
to the memory of
Henry John, son of John Roberts
Collector of Customs, who died
at Santa Maura, on the 10th day
of August 1845

14.

Sacred
to the memory of
Mary, wife of Alfred Dillon,
Engineer-master of the Steam Dredger,
Pelican, who departed this life on
the 11th May 1852, aged 27 years

15.

To the memory of
James Edwards, Lieutenant HBM's
9th Regiment of Foot, who was accidentally
drowned in the Gulph (sic) of Arta on the 3 July 186,
aged 23 years

16.
On the ramparts of the fort, near the flagstaff a monument was erected by order of HE General James Campbell, HM's Civil Commissioner and Commander-in-Chief of the Forces in the Ionian and Adriatic Islands, as a mark of his esteem and regard:

> AD 1815
> Sacred
> to the memory of
> Major-General Davis, Adjutant
> General of HBM's forces in Sicily
> who, on his return from Greece
> died at Santa Maura on the
> 26th December 1813, in the 45 year
> of his age

ROMAN CATHOLIC CEMETERY, SANTA MAURA (LEVKAS)

1.

Sacred
to the memory of
Margaret Wright, who
departed this life in 1844, aged 42
and Color Sergeant John Wright, who
departed this life on the 17 January 1843
aged 38 years

2.

To the memory of
Corporal Patrick O'Leary of the 76 Battn
who departed this life on the 18th June
1848, aged 30 years

3.

To the memory of
John Sonol Michael Coltherts, aged 35

4.

To the memory of
Thomas Cuddiley, Pvt 11 Regiment, who departed
this life on the 9 September 1833, aged
28 years

5.

Sacred
to the memory of
John Bowdedge, Private 11 Regiment
who departed this life on the 3 January
1832, aged 22 years

6.
                    Gloria in Excelsis Deus Gloria
                              IHS
               In front of this stone lays the
                        remains of
               Mary Reardaut alias Cahill,
       wife of Sergeant Armourer Jeremiah
      Reardaut, 11th Regiment of Foot, who
       departed this life on the 27 October
                  1831, aged 23 years

7.
                       To the memory of
Thomas Ash, who departed this life on the 2nd August 1831, aged 23 years

There are seven more graves with inscriptions that were illegible, and another seven more without tombstones.

ENGLISH CEMETERY, ITHACA

This cemetery adjoins the Greek Churchyard.

1.

In memory of
Sergt J Brogden, age 28
Corpl T Crowther, age 24
Corpl H Hale, age 26
Corpl D Stanyard, age 23
No 3 Company
HM 2nd Battn 9th Regiment
Drowned at Ithaca
February 28th, 1864
Erected by their Comrades
In the midst of Life we are in Death

2.

To the memory of
Private Benjamin Cook
No 8 Company
2nd Battalion, 2nd Queen's Royals
who died at Ithaca,
on the 2nd May 1862,
aged 24 years
This stone is erected by the
Officers and Men
of his Company

3.

Sacred
to the memory
of
Corporal J Armour
No 10 Battn, 6th Brigade, RI Artillery
who departed this life 18 July 1861,
aged 32 years
This stone was erected by
the Non-Comd Officers &
Privates of the Detachment
of HBM, 1st Battn, 9th Regiment
Also one Serjt RI Artillery &
one RI Engineers, by whom
he was much esteemed and
his loss deeply regretted

4.

Sacred

to the memory of
Private Edward Lund
late of the Vth Fusiliers
who departed this life
27th Novr 1840
in the 35th year of his age
This stone is erected by
his Comrade soldiers as
a small tribute of regard
and esteem
When heaven permits a good
man's fall, the loss lamented is by all
A faithful soldier's comrade dear
such was the man that lieth here

5.

IHS
Sacred
to the memory of Jane Cunningham
who departed this life on
the 2nd of October 1845
aged 23 years
This stone was erected by her beloved husband
Patrick Cunningham, 9th Regt
as a testimony of his
love and esteem
Requiscat in pace, Amen

6.

Sacred
to
the memory of Samuel Ching
Seaman of HM Brig *Weazle*,
who departed this life on
the 5th of Augt 1841
This stone is erected
as a mark of respect by
his shipmates

7.

Sacred
to
the memory of Thos Roscoe
Seaman of HM Brig *Weazle*
who departed this life on
the 6th of Augt 1841
This stone is erected
as a mark of respect by
his shipmates

8.

Sacred
to the memory of
Mary Ann McAvoy
the second beloved daughter of
Patrick Louis McAvoy
Royal Artillery
who departed this life
the 28 October 1839,
aged 7 months
Hark, a voice divides the Sky.
Happy are the faithful dead
In the Lord who sweetly die.
They from all their toils are freed.

9.

Sacred
to the memory of
Henry Dyart, late
Gunner of Major Thos
Grantham's Company
Royal Arty, who departed
this life 21st Decr 1839,
aged 31 years
This stone is erected by his comrade soldiers
as a tribute of respect and esteem

10.
To the memory
of
John McDonald
who died 3rd January
1852
aged 11 months

11.
Sacred
to the memory
of
Donald Macdonald, private soldier, 1st Battn, 60th Royal Rifle Corps, who
departed this life, 16 January 1839, aged 29 years
deeply regretted by
all who knew him
This tablet is erected by his Officer, Non-Com'd Officers and Comrades stationed
on Ithaca on the 16th January 1839 as a
token of their regard and esteem

12. [Plain stone with cross]
Sacred
to the memory of
William Dowling, private soldier, 1st Battn, 60th Royal Rifle Corps who
departed this life 4th February 1839, aged 36, deeply regretted by
all who knew him
This tablet is
erected by his Officer, Non-Comm'd
Officers and Comrades as a testimony of their esteem and regard.

13.
IHS
Sacred to the memory
of
Lawrence Byrnes
private soldier of the
97th Regt
who departed this life
on the 16th Decr 1841
aged 21 years
This small tribute of respect
is erected by the Non-Com'd Officers
and Private Soldiers of the Comp^y
to which he belonged as a testimony due to a faithful and
good soldier

14.
Sacred
to the memory of
Charles Johnly Acht
only child of
Captn C F Tuckey
41st Welch Regiment
born at Ithaca, April 25th 1852
died 4 [?] October 1852
Suffer little children to come unto Me. Luke xviii 15

15.
To
the memory
of John Hercules Spence
son of John Spence
Color Sergt 41st Regt
who departed this
life on the 3rd Oct
1852
aged 1 year 6 months
It is but the voice that Jesus sends to call them to his arms

16.
Sacred
to
the memory
of
Robert Bidwell, Pt Soldier
of the Cr Comp 41 Reg who was
drowned on the 7th March 1852
aged 27 years. This St-
one is erected to his Memory by his comrades who
deeply deplore his loss

17.
Sacred to the memory
of
Private James Bird of No 1
Company, 31st Regiment who
suddenly departed this life
on the 18 of July 1853, aged 31 years
He served in the East Indies
from the 19th Nov 1841 to the 2nd
Augt 1846 and was present at
the following general
engagements viz at
Moudke, Ferozeshuhur,
Alewal and Sobroan, for
which he received a
silver medal and three clasps
This stone is erected by
the Non-Comd Officers
and Privates of No 1
Company 31st Regt as a
Token of Esteem and Regard

18.
Sacred
to
the memory of
John Thomas Wheat
son of John and Joyce Wheat, first King's Own
Stafford Militia
who departed this life
7th August 1856,
aged 9 months
This stone was erected by de[?sire]
of the above-named corps as a token
of respect
Suffer little Children to come unto
me, for of such is the Kingdom of Heaven

19.

Sacred to the memory
IHS
of Private Patrick Kemmingham
late of the 19th Regiment
who departed this life
Feby 23, 1844, in the 38th year of his age
This stone is erected by the
Officers, Non-Commd Officers and
Comrades as a token of their
esteem and regard

20.

Sacred
to
the memory
of
William Andw Elliott
died Octr 26th, 1847
aged 2 yrs and 10 months

21.

Sacred to the memory
of
William Hartell
Pt Soldier of the
Lt Compy
16th Regt
who departed this
life on the 26th
Febuary [sic] 1851
age 30 years
This stone is erected
to his memory by is
comrades who deeply
deplore his loss

22.

Sacred to the
memory of
Benjamin Hawes,
who died at Ithaca, March 28, 1864, aged 4 days
Suffer little Children to come unto me and forbid them not

BRITISH CEMETERY, CEPHALONIA

These notes taken from the British Cemetery by J D Waller of Alderney, Channel Islands, were first published in *The Manchester Genealogist* Vol 25/2 (April 1989), p20. The listing gave only bare details from gravestones and they have been set out here in the traditional manner. Thus although the wording of the actual inscription may be different, the genealogical information is accurate.

1.
Lt Col Thomas Wright,
CO of Light Infantry,
died 19 Sept 1824

2.
Arch McAllister,
2nd Bat, Rifle Brigade,
died 21 Nov 1835, aged 29.

3.
NCOs and Privates of the 1st King's Own Staffordshire Regiment

Sgt George Grocott	25 Oct 1855
Cpl George Simpson	29 Sept 1855
Pte George Bennett	28 Aug 1855
Pte John Moran	1 Oct 1855
Pte Augustine Cannon	3 Oct 1855
Pte James Evans	11 Oct 1855
Pte Edward Chown	13 Oct 1855
Pte George Hill	15 Oct 1855
Pts Samuel Morgan	22 Oct 1855
Pte Samuel Lloyd	23 Oct 1855
Pte Samuel Hartshorn	24 Oct 1855
Pte Moses Brettel	26 Oct 1855
Pte George F Hutton	2 Nov 1855
Pte Thomas Morgan	2 Nov 1855
Pte Joseph Bratt	16 Nov 1855
Pte James Mellor	19 Nov 1855
Pte Conman Welsh	21 Nov 1855
Pte Jeremiah Devannaoh	27 Nov 1855
Pte Daniel Dix	29 Nov 1855
Pte George Bate	16 Dec 1855
Pte Thomas Deer	11 Feb 1856
Pte James Caldwell	16 April 1856

4.
In memory of men of 36 Regt who died of cholera between 11th and 21st
September 1850
Pte James Mudd 33
Pte Wm Bateman 30
Pte James Nicholls 36
Dr Wm Galloway 26
Pte Thomas Guy 21
Pte George Ryder 22
L/C Richard Carpenter 21
Pte Wm Shimmons 13 July 1850, aged 22 of fever
Walter Wm Ford, bugler of HMS *Suffolk*, 18 Sept 1906, aged 17.
Capt Arthur Onslow Creighton, 36 Regt, died of fever, 3 Sept 1848, in 26th year.

5.
Privates of 5 Coy, 36 Regt who died of cholera, Aug-Sept 1830
Michael Doolon aged 28 years, 8 months
Robert Haifron aged 32 years, 6 months
Charles Summerfield aged 30 years, 5 months
Thomas Morgan aged 25 years, 9 months
George Morgan aged 38 years, 9 months
James Ives aged 21 years, 6 months

6.
Arthur Edwin Dawson,
of HMS *Marlborough*,
fell from aloft in the execution of his duty
and died 4 June 1862, aged 18,

7.
Pte James Lewis,
2nd Bn, 4th King's Own Regt
died 28 Feb 1862,
aged 25 years, 11 months.

8.
Pte M Ballaam,
68th Light Infantry

9.
Sarah Jeffs,
wife of Sgt Major J Jeffs,
died 10 Feb 1867, aged 53

10.
>
> Jeanette,
> wife of John M Lindsey
> Deputy Assistant Commissary General
> died 7 Aug 1861,
> aged 27

11.
>
> Emmanuel J C Toole
> son of Eman and Eliza Toole,
> 2nd Batn, 1st Foot,
> died 3 Oct 1854, aged 4 years
> Also
> his sister
> Mary L E Toole,
> died 24 Feb 1855, aged 2 years

12.
>
> John Huddleston Esq
> Capt, 18 Regt
> died of cholera, 12 Oct 1850, aged 64

13.
>
> Erected by
> Thomas McCammon of Belfast
> in memory of his eldest son
> John
> who died 1 April 1845, aged 19

14.
>
> Charles Davis Esq
> who died 6 Sept 1858, aged 65

15.
>
> Erected by
> Lieut Col Richard Fred Hill
> in memory of his only son
> Henry
> who died 29 Nov 1838
> aged 17 months

16.
George William F Darrah,
Son of Lieut Col Darrah
born 5 Nov 1843
died 14 Feb 1846

17.
Emma Louisa Woodley,
born 6 April 1865
died 2 Dec 1877

18.
George Sparkes,
Engineer, HMS *Alexandra*,
died 31 Oct 1885, aged 31

19.
E A Toole
5 Nov 1823 – 12 July 1906

20.
James Toole
1863-1925

21.
Marietta Toole
27 Aug 1835 – 29 Nov 1895

22.
John Aug Toole
1 Feb 1860 – 16 Nov 1922

23.
John Aug Toole
died 1929, aged 37 years

24.
George Aug Toole
died 25 Feb 1877, aged 64 years

25.
William Anthony Toole
9 July 1870 – Dec 1877

26.
Marietta J Toole
died 17 June 1936, aged 3

27.
Allig Peter Toole
26 April 1839 – 15 Feb 1927

28.
George A Toole
died 28 Feb 1877

29.
Anne A Toole
died 2 April 1900

30.
Mary Saunders
died 7 Feb 1800 [1900?]

31.
Pte John Anderson
died 11 Dec 1813, in his 30th year

32.
Sgt Thomas Harvey
19th Regt of Foot
died 21 May 1843, aged 33 years
after 16 years in the Regt

33.
Leading Stoker Edward Snell
of HMS *Chamois*
died 29 Sept 1904, aged 34

34.
In memory of
Sgt David Doudie, of
91st Regt
who died 22 Nov 1857, aged 36 &
Eliz his widow erected this stone

35.
Matilda Mary Ann,
wife of Rev John Buchanan
died 9 Sept 1837, in her 22nd year

36.
Pte G A Tuthill,
9th Regt,
died 13 Sept 1863
aged 35

ENGLISH CEMETERY, ZANTE

This cemetery, also known as St John's Cemetery, is said to have first opened in 1650. In the 1930s it was in the charge of the British Vice-Consul for Morea and Zante. In 1932 the following gravestones were recorded as being still extant: 1, 4-13, 15-16, 18-26, 28-33, 37-41, 43-46, 48-50. In the same year some of the surviving graves from the Protestant and the Catholic cemeteries in Zante were moved to the English Cemetery.

1. [On a slab of black marble]
> Clemens Harby, eqves Avratvs
> Consvl Anglican in Peloponeso
> Et Insvla Zacynthi
> Anno Domini 1689

Sir Clement Harby, son of Clement Harby of London, was educated at Merchant Taylors' School in 1620. He was Consul at Morea and knighted at Whitehall in 1669. Harby was regarded as a formidable diplomat and consul during the 1670s, and many of his papers are held at the Public Record Office, London.

2. [Large stone altar-tomb with incised arm, probably formerly containing a bronze coat-of-arms]
> Sacred to the memory
> of
> Margaret Emma
> daughter of
> Joseph and Mary Thomas
> Died 30th January
> MDCCCXVII
> aged 18

3. [Small stone stele above inscription]
> IHS
> Here lyeth the body of the Infant child
> of
> Major-General Airey
> Commander, His Britt Majesty's troops
> in the Ionian liberated Islands
> and
> Catherine, his wife
> who departed this life on the 5th day of
> November MDCCCXII
> aged three months and six days

Catherine was the third daughter of Richard Talbot who married Baroness Talbot de Malahide. Sir George Airey, born in 1761, married Catherine in Oct 1797, and they had several children. Airey, a career soldier, accompanied General Fox to Sicily in 1805 and commanded a brigade in Sicily in 1810. Two years later he was appointed Commandant of British Forces in the Ionian Islands. He died 15 Feb 1833, and Catherine died 13 May 1852.

4. [Altar-shaped tomb with inscription on white marble slab]
Sacred to the memory
of
Sarah, daughter of Surgeon Martin
73rd Regiment
who died in the Castle of Zante
on the 29th June 1835
aged 18 years

5. [White marble slab on the ground]
Sacred
to the memory
of Anthony John, son of
Benjamin Kane
and Caroline, his wife
who died on the 5th of July 1825
aged 14 months

6. [Plain stone cross]
Patrick Stuart
Thomas
eldest son of
Charles S Thomas
and Mary his wife
died April 11th 1865, aged 20 years
Blessed are the pure in heart, for they
shall see God
Matth v ch 9 ver

7. [Plain headstone]
Sacred to the memory
of
Edward George Gray
Ensign in Her Majesty's 76th Regt who departed
this life on the 28th
July 1848, aged 22 years
2 months, second son of Thomas Gray and
Jane Bertram, his wife
of Roseville, in the
Island of Jeray

8. [Triangular stone monument with fluted columns at the three corners, surmounted with an urn having a marble slab in front]

>The 90th Light Infantry
>to their
>Esteemed and lamented
>Adjutant
>Lieut Hector Munroe
>who died on the 3rd Aug
>1828
>aged 34 years

9. [Low altar with inscription on the top]

>Sacred
>to the memory of
>Frances Eliza
>the infant daughter
>of William and Ellen Kirby
>died 26 November 1841
>aged 18 months

10. [Large marble slab]

>To
>the memory of
>Luke Whitney Esq
>late Surgeon
>90th Light Infantry
>who died
>5th January 1825,
>aged 37 years

11. [Plain stone altar-tomb with white marble slab, let in at the top]

>Sacred
>to
>the memory of
>Henry Thos Harris
>of
>HM Ship *Caledonia*
>who was killed by
>falling from the
>rigging at Zante on
>the 2nd October 1835
>aged 29 years

12. [Plain sloping slab]
Hic jacet
D Alexander Dodsworth
Virtute moribus doctrina
perinsignia Apoplexia A vivis ereptus
Die XXII Octobris MDCCCIX [or MDCCCXIX]
Ætatis anæ Annorum LXVI
Præceptor Comitis Petri Macri
Comitis Basilli filii
Lugente tota familia
et ipsius Expensis
tumalatus
M'signum obsequii
et perpetuae gratitudimis
pater et filiss
exerunt
DOMP
Anno A.N.D. MDCCCIX

13. [Large monument surmounted by a sarcophagus with marble slab on front]
To the memory
of the wife and child
of Lieut Colonel Gubbins, 75th Regt
Zante, 6th September 1820

14.[Marble monument with inscription, engraved with a rose, and there was a vase under the poem]
Frederick Henry Clark
Born Zante, June 1839
Died October 3rd 1844
The lovely bud, so young, so fair
Call'd hence by early doom,
Just came to show how sweet a flower
In paradise would Bloom

15. [Curious triangular monument of black-veined marble under a canopy supported by four columns. Inscription repeated on reverse side in Latin.]
Here lyeth interred the body of James Paul, Esq, His Brittanick (sic)
Majesty's Colonel in the Morea, Cerigo, Zante, Cefalonia
and Corfu who dyed the 27th of August 1728 in the 75 year
of his age & the 39 of His Consulship. Much lamented by every-
body & generally beloved for his integrity &c and a benefactor
to the island

Zante: English Cemetery

16. [Plain stone headstone]
To the memory of
Stephen Dawson Esq
of Albemarle Street
London
Born 21st Novr 1814
Died 6th Aug 1838
And was here interred

17.
Sacred
to the memory of ---
son of
F Craig, and of Martha, his wife who died 19th July 1820
aged – months & 3 days, also
W ---, his brother who died
-- 1820, aged 3 years
1 month & 8 days
O Brother dear ...

18. [Stone altar with festoons round base and inscription above]
Sacred
to the memory of
Thomas Parnell Esqr
Dutch Consul
at Patrass
who died on this island
Nov 5th 1821
aged 33 years
His affectionate sister Olivia Lecazza has erected this tomb

19. [Handsome altar-tomb supported by four lions' heads and paws, and above inscription two coats of arms.]
DOM
Cineres
Danielis Moore
From Brit Rege
Rei Mero cvr
apvd zacynthios
pracf
QVA XL D XXIV
chareq coni
Valententinae holmes
QVA XXIX M III

20. [Sloping altar-tomb surrounded by iron railing]
Sacred
to the memory of
Colquhoun Grant Esq MD
Surgeon to the Forces
An old and meritorious officer
who died at Zante
on the 2nd January 1848
in the 63rd year of his age
This stone is erected
by his bereaved widow
and afflicted family

21. [Scroll shaped altar-tomb of inscribed white marble; coat of arms above inscription: dog's head above a helmet]
DOM
Lecinere di
Samuel Hayward
Da so Majeste Britannica
Elefto 1735
Console
di Zante, Corfu, Cefalonia, Itache
& territori tutti serenissima
republica di Venezia in Levanti
con
la provincia della Morea
Natalico &c

22. [Plain altar-tomb]
Sacred to the memory
of
John Simpson Esqr
Deputy Assistant
Commissary General
who died on the 20th Octr
1833,
aged 44 years

23. [Plain altar-tomb with sloping stone slab, inscription in lead letters; above the inscription a cross and leaves are engraved; below are some military emblems]

In loving memory
of
F L [or Co] Chiaranda
Assistant Commissary General
who died 22d November 1856 [or 1855]
aged 66 years
This monument is erected by his daughter
The memory of the just is blessed.

24. [Plain altar-tomb]
Sacred to the memory
of
Color Sergt John Rey
No 2 Company 7th Batt
Royal Artillery
who departed this life
on the 18th of Augt 1838
aged 37 years
Here, comrades, stay and shed a tear,
A soldier brave lies buried here.
Soon hurried to his parents' dust,
At noon in health, at night a corpse
Recent in time, make no delay,
For I in haste was call'd away.
Sweet Partner of my life, farewell,
To Heaven I soar with Christ to dwell
This stone was erected
by the Company
to which he belonged as a mark of the
high esteem in which he was held
as a
brother soldier

25. [Small sloping slab let into a stone, above the inscription a wreath of primroses with the inscription carved; there are reversed torches tied with ribbon engraved below.]

Annie
daughter of John and Eliza Lindsey
Born at Zante 11th June 1856
Died 31st July 1857 [or 1859]

26. [Upright monument of white marble surmounted by a cross.]
Sacred
to the memory
of
George Dodd Clark
Born Zante 15th Febry 1830
Died Zante 30th Jany 1849
For as in Adam all die, even so in
Christ shall all be made alive – 1 Cor xv 22
Blessed are the pure in heart
for they shall see God – St Math v 8

27. [Small stone altar-tomb]
Sacred
to the memory of
Arthur Ernest,
infant child of
Lt Col R F Hill
and Maria Jane, his wife
who died at Zante,
November 19th 1848
aged 6 months

28. [Marble headstone with pediment, on the pediment there is a cross on a rock]
Sacred
to the
memory
of
Captain
John Taylor
who departed
this life
March 26, 1843
aged 35 years

29. [An altar-tomb with white marble slab, engraved]

> Sacred
> to the memory
> of
> Ann Miles, wife of Lieut Francis Miles
> of the 8th Regt of Foot
> who departed this life
> the 18th day of August 1821
> aged 23 years
> Also
> to the memory of George
> their infant son who died
> 4 days after the above,
> aged 8 months

30. [Sloping slab]

> Sacred
> to the memory of
> James Tennent Esqr, Depy Asst Commisy Genl
> who died at Zante
> on the 14th Septr
> 1844

31. [Small altar-tomb]

> In memory of
> the infant son
> of Captn Fras Marsh, 11th Reg
> and Isabella, his wife
> who died Febry the 12th 1834
> aged 3 months & 25 days

32. [Plain altar-tomb with panelled sides, inscribed with lead letters]

> Sacred
> to the memory of
> Sophia Vernon, wife of
> Major Henry Vernon of the
> Thirty-sixth Regiment of
> Foot who departed this life
> the 18th day of April 1821
> aged 36 years
> Not lost, but gone before

Henry Vernon might have been the soldier killed in the clash between peasants and the crew of a grounded Turkish brig (Pratt, *Britain's Greek Empire*, p121).

33. [Large altar-tomb, with the inscription repeated in Greek]
Sacred
to the memory
of Olivia Lee
of Old Charlton, in Kent
the werthy (sic) and affectionate
wife of John Legazza of Zante
who lived by the will
of the Lord years 50
died the 27th September 1848

34. [Sloping stone]
Sacred
to
the memory
of
Sarabella Chiaranda
who died in Zante
on
the 11 of December 1843

35. [Large altar-tomb with skull and cross-bones engraved above the inscription and shield for arms below]
Here lyeth interred the body
of David Paul, son of James Paul Esq,
Her Britannick Consul at Zante & C who departed
this life on the XXIV Octobr in the
year of our Lord MDCCXIII of the small-pox, aged XVII years

36. [Upright stone]
--
departed this life at Zante
on the 9th –
aged 27 years

37. [Sloping stone, with biblical quotation in Greek]

Sacred
to the memory of Mary Croggan
wife of W O Croggan,
Wesleyan Missionary
She died August 5th 1830,
aged 31
Here also lie the remains
of S A Croggan, their daughter
who died November 25th 1827
Also the remains of two babes,
One was buried June 8th 1829
and the other with his Mother, August 6th 1830
Blessed are the dead which die in the Lord – Rev xiv 13

38. [An altar-tomb]

Sacred
to the memory of
Elizabeth,
wife of Revd Isaac Loundes
Protestant Missionary
She departed this life
Jan 15 1821, aged 30 years
in the joyful anticipation of
a blessed resurrection
to eternal life
through the redemption of
Christ Jesus
John W [I?] Loundes
son of the above, died July 25, 1821
aged 8 months
Mary H Loundes
her daughter

[illegible]

39. [Upright stone]

Sacred
to the memory of
John Harvey
Master Mariner of Torquay, England
who died in Zante, May 1, 1818
aged 31 years
leaving a wife and three daughters
to lament his loss
But thanks be to God which giveth us the Victory through our Lord Jesus Christ;
therefore my beloved brethren, be ye steadfast, unmoveable, always abounding
in the work of the Lord, forasmuch that ye know that your labour is not in vain in the
Lord – 1 Cor Chap xv v 57, 58

40. [Altar-tomb with inscription, formerly in lead letters, now gone]

Sacred
to the memory of
Mr Joseph Kemp
late Quarter Master
of the 36th regiment
who departed this life
the 2d day of January 1821
aged 46 years
This stone is erected
as a mark of esteem
by his brother Officers
Boast not thyself of to-morrow,
For thou knowest not
what a day may bring forth
Pro 27th Chap 1st Ver

41. [Altar-tomb]

Sacred
to the memory
of Maria Matthews
wife of
Thos B White
who departed this life
12th Septr 1888
aged 45 years

42. [Flat black marble slab; with the same inscription in Italian below English-language inscription]
Here lies interred
The Honest Merchant & the generally be
Mr Robert Anderson, a British subject
who departed this life the 16 March 1747,
aged 73 years

43. [Pyramidal stone]
Erected
by
John and Sophia Woodley
of
Zante
1841
[On front side]
Denis Rowland
departed this life
4th October 1830
aged 2 years

44. [Sloping white marble slab]
In memory of
Jane
widow of late Thomas Broughton
who departed this life
at Zante 14 March 1863,
aged 67 years
Also
of Angelo and Samuel
infant children
of John and Sophia Woodley

45. [Black marble slab on sloping base, above inscription a cross, below a skull and cross-bones]
Here lies the body of John
Ferguson, Mercht
who departed this life the
30 July 1753
in the 35th year
of his age

46. [Sloping white marble slab]
To the memory
of
Robert Bachelor Sargint
who departed this life
on the 13th day of March
in the year of our Lord 1852
aged 81

47. [Sloping slab of white marble]
Maria Katherine Lountzei
Born in Venice, 4 Feb 1776
Died in Zante, 8 Oct 1850

48. [Altar-tomb with large slab and coat of arms above the inscription]
DOM
Thomæ Cordell Angli
illustres cineres
hoc tumulo
spiritus
coelo
semper gaudet
natalium nobilitata morum suavitate
exornavit
Quem si dira mors immature feriit
mature superi rapuere
nam
florenti adhuc setate
seniorum in mercatura experientiam
uon sorte sed virtute
pretergressus
perpetuum sinceræ negotiationis documentum
reliquit
hinc
coelesti non terrestri patria
dignus
annos suos vitae XXXVII
clausit MDCLXXXVI
et
amutissimi fratris pietate
hic
revixit
MDCLXXXVII

49. [On a platform above a plain slab]
Sacred
to the memory
of
Sylvia Olivia Narcissa Catherine
daughter of Thomas Lee Parnell Esq
of Charlton, Kent
and the beloved wife
of
Dionysius C Loverdo of Zante
who departed this life
on the 24th July 1863,
aged 46 years

50. [Recumbent cross, on a base]
Sacred to the memory of
Augustus E H Ansell, Major, 4th the King's Own Regiment
Departed this life, 6th Deceber (sic) 1862
Erected to his memory by his brother officers

51.
Hier ruht in Gett
fern von seinen Lieben
der Lehrer
Hermann Gall
aus Halle spi Königreich Preussen
Geboren 2 September 1825
Gest d 4 November 1862

52. [Lone stone monument]
Sacred
to the memory
of
John Smith, late Corp
in His Britannic Majesty's
35th Regiment
A Soldier truly respected
A man much beloved
Alas
A soldier death snatched
Zante
on the 2nd day of Septr 1812
& in the 30 year of his age
Leaving behind a
tender wife & child to mourn their loss. Life's short span
forbids us to indulge
in distant
expectation

PROTESTANT CEMETERY, ZANTE

This cemetery used to be on the Psiloma Road. In 1932 the cemetery was closed and many surviving graves were moved to the English Cemetery (see p179). Those from the following list known to have been moved are: 1-2, 4-5, 7, 9-10.

1. [Plain white marble slab]
Sacred to the memory
of
2nd Class Instr of Musketry
William Brown
1st Bn, 9th Regt
who departed this life
23rd [or 28th] January 1864
aged 37 years, 10 months
This stone
was erected by his comrade Serjeants
as a token of respect

2. [Plain stone with a Maltese cross above inscription]
Sacred
to the memory
of George Roberts
who departed this
life, 20th Febry 1859, aged one year and
ten months
son of George and Mary
Roberts of HM's 1st Batt^{on} 14 Regt

3. [Plain stone with cross above inscription]
Sacred
to the memory
of Richd Thos Hill
son of Colour Serjeant Hill
1st Batt, 14 Regt and Hanora, his wife
who died at
Zante, 21 Dec 185[9?],
aged 12 months

4. [Plain headstone inscribed 1st Bn, 14th Foot above a cross. Inscription below the Cross]

Sacred
to the memory
of Rd Wm Moss
son of
Colr Sergt Rd Moss &
Elizabeth, his wife
He departed this life on
the 20th Sepr 1859
aged 1 year & 4 months
Not lost, but gone before

5. [Recumbent headstone of red marble; second inscription on small stone]

Sacred
to the memory
of
Joseph Pitman Esq
Duke of Lancaster's Own Rt
who died at Zante
the 21st of Nov 1855, aged 23 years
This headstone is erected by
his brother officers as a mark
of their
respect & esteem

Also the remains of
Jane, their infant daughter

6. [Altar-tomb on four columns]

Beneath this tomb are
deposited the remains of Richd Wilm
and Isabella Hamat [?], son & daughter
of Sert Jo^n Roberts and Letitia, his wife
75th Regt, the former departed this life
on the 8 May 1836, aged 7 months
& the latter on the 23d June 1836, aged 21 [?]
years & 8 months at Zante

7. [Plain altar-tomb with a small cross engraved above inscription]
Sacred
to the memory
of
Sara Jane Weir
daughter of C Serjt Geo Weir
and Sarah
1st Batt, 14 Regiment
His wife,
who died in Zante
the 24 [or 28] Oct 1858
aged 18 months
Also
John Weir
died
19 July 1859,
age 1 day

8. [Low headstone with shaped top]
Sacred
to
the memory of Charles Cox, 41 Regt
who departed this life 10 Sept 1831, aged 13 years & 6 months
Here lies one fair boy who left his native isle
Buoyant with hope, his heart free from guile
Now lies at rest, his youthful spirits fled,
Far, far, from home he rests his little head.

9. [Low headstone]
Sacred to the memory
of
Ellenor Daniel, wife of
Gunner Charles Daniel
of the 7th Battn, Royal Art
who departed this life
on the 27th of Aug [or Oct] 1838,
aged 34 years

10. [Plain headstone]
Sacred to the memory
of
Frederick Dedrick
late Serjeant of the
band of the 11th Regiment
of British Infantry
He was born in Meltick in Prussia
in the year 1789 and departed
this life on the 23 Octr 1834 [or 1831]

11. [Plain headstone]
Sacred to the memory
of
Serjt William Guttridge
Late of the 11th Regt of Foot
who departed this life on the
19 day of Decr 1833, aged 51 years
This stone was erected by the
non-commissioned officers of
the above Regt as a token of their esteem for a comrade

12. [Small headstone]
Sacred
to the memory
of
Michael Hunt
38th Rt

13. [Headstone]
Sacred
to
the memory of
James Byrne, Seaman of HMS
Revenge, who died on the 3rd October 1835,
aged 22 years
In that dread moment, how in frantic soul
… of her clay tenement
[fifteen lines illegible]

14. [Small recumbent stone]
To the memory
of
Eliza Unwin, 1854

CATHOLIC CEMETERY, ZANTE

This cemetery used to be on the Psiloma Road next to the Protestant Cemetery (see p194). In 1932 the cemetery was closed and many surviving graves were moved to the English Cemetery. Those from the following list known to have been moved are: 2-7, 10-11. It appears that 4 may have been erected at the English Cemetery in two parts.

1. [Latin inscription, almost obliterated.]

2. [Altar-tomb]
Sacred
to the memory
of M A Donting
wife of M Donting
Xth Royal Lancashire Militia
who departed this life
on the 22nd October 1855
aged 33 years, 6 months
leaving a disconsolate
husband
and – [7?] children to lament their loss
May she rest in peace

3. ['Interesting monument' in 'old style' with death's head and cross-bones at base.]
IHS
Erected to the memory
of
Elizabeth Sullivan
who departed this life
on the 9th day of April
in the year of our Lord 1830
aged 25 years
In dust comingled here, Mother & Child,
A sad retreat in this lone home enjoy profound,
In earth their bodies to rest beguiled,
Extatic (sic) bliss their souls in heaven have found.
This tomb is erected by her disconsolate
husband T Sullivan, 10th Regt of Foot

4. [Altar-tomb]
Sacred
to the memory
of
Geo Welby, who died 5th Dec 1858
Wm Slackyard, 21st Jany 1859
Thos Shea, 3rd Novr 1859
Daniel Hogan, 7th Decr 1860 [1861]
2nd Battalion, 9th Regiment of Foot
No 9 Company
Erected by their comrades as a mark of esteem

5. [Large fallen headstone]
Sacred to the memory
[of]
John Graney
late School Mr Serj
in HM 10th Rt of Foot
who departed this life
the 17th of June 1831
in the 27th year of his
age
This stone is erected
as a token of esteem
by his Comrade Serjts

6. [Headstone]
To
the memory of the late Serjeant John Henry
20 years Master of
the band of the 36th Regiment who
departed this life the 18th day
of February 1821
aged 37 years

7. [Headstone]
Gloria in Excelsis Deo
IHS
In front of this stone lies
the remains of Serjeant
James O'Connor, late Orderly
Room Clerk at the 11th Regt
of foot who departed this
life on the 12th of May 1833
aged 39 years
This stone is erected by the Non-
Commissioned Officers of the
above Regt as a token of their
esteem and very great regard

8. [Altar-tomb]
IHS
Sacred to the memory
of
Denis Reardan
son of Jeremiah Reardan
Armourer Serjeant, 11th Regt
who departed this life
19th of January
1835
aged 18 years
Resquiescat in pace
Amen

9. [Altar-tomb]
IHS
†
Sacred to the memory
of Elizabeth Moran,
wife of Serjt Nicholas Moran
1st Battalion, 14th Regiment
who departed this life at
Zante 11th Jany 1859, aged
34 years. Erected by her
surviving husband
Resquiescat in pace
Amen

10. [Altar-tomb]
Erected
by the Serjeants
of the
31st Regiment
as a tribute of respect
to the memory
of Colr Serjt J Foley
late of the
31st Regiment
who died at Zante
12th August
1853 [1855]
aged 23 years

11. [Pyramidal monument with inscription on one end]
Sacred
to the memory of Sarah,
wife of Cr Sert W Kerrigan, 91 Regt
who died at Zante
on the 27th February 1858
aged 25 years
leaving her two infant
children to deplore their loss
Erected by the NC Officers & men
of No 1 Compy as a mark of respect

12. [In a wall, a small marble slab]
†
Sacred to the memory
of
Pte William Hayes
1st Bn, 9th Regt
who departed this life
25th January 1864
aged 31 years, 4 months
May his soul rest in peace
This stone
was erected by his comrades of
No 7 Company
as a token of respect

GENERAL CEMETERY, ZANTE

1. [Black board completely obliterated]

2.
Sacred to the memory
of
Robert Mitchell
of HMS *Inflexible*
who was killed from falling from aloft
at Zante
on Thursday, April 10th 1884,
aged 18 years
A sudden change, I in a moment fell,
I had not time to bid my friends farewell;
Think this not strange, death happens unto all,
This day was mine, tomorrow you may fall
This stone was erected by the officers and
men of HMS *Inflexible*

3.
SS *Columba*
2.10.89
Owen Hughes
aged 47
Rest in peace

4.
Sacred to the memory of
William Foote
of Brig *Martha Edmunds*
Born at Sheldon, Devon
1839
died at Zante ... 1886

5.
Sacred
to the memory of
Ada Ellen Short
died Feb 13th 187
aged 16 months

Zante: General Cemetery

6.
To the memory of
Christine Beveridge Leighton
dearly beloved wife
of
David Leighton
who departed this life
the 13th of May 1883
aged 31 years
Deeply regretted by all

7. [On the right hand side of the entrance to the cemetery]
To the memory of
Andrew
son of William Archer & Giovanna, his wife
died 27 Nov 1855,
aged 11 years

8. [Northern end of cemetery]
In memory of
Edward Hayes
Born in Smyrna 16th Jan 1800
Died at Zante 27th Novr 1875
Patient in tribulation

9.
In memory of
Catherine Mary
the beloved child
of
Richard & Clara Sargint
died 6th August 1875
aged 2 years
He shall gather the lambs in His arms
& carry them in His bosom
Isaiah xl, v 11

10.
To the memory of
George Stevens, Esquire
died on 12th July 1869

In memory
of
R C M Stevens
Born 9th Oct 1817
Died 5th July 1879

11. [Eastern side of cemetery]
Sacred to the memory of
Samuel Barff
Born at Wakefield
7th August 1793
Died at Zante 3rd Sept 1880
After a residence in this island of 64 years
Blessed is he that considereth the poor
and needy: the Lord shall deliver him in the
time of trouble   Psalm xli 1

12. [Southern side of cemetery; inscription in Greek]
John Lindsey
Manager of the Ionian Bank
born 30 Aug – 11 September 1820
died 25 December 1873 – 8 January 1874

ENGLISH CEMETERY, CERIGO

There are two memorials on the wall of the medieval church (1-2). The remainder were in the cemetery but some are now in the Hora Museum, possibly moved there after the earthquake of 1953.

1. [North wall of church]

        Sacred
    to the memory
          of
     John Smith
Pensioner and Waterloo man
Ended his days on the 2nd of
  April 1876, at the age of
      84 years

2. [South wall of church]

         DOM
AD III Daloysius Cortesius
hujus Cerighi Forti icii Gub
ernator ad millri dangelle de
angelis dilectiss vxori anno
ætatis sue xxv xii Augusti
MDCXXIII mortue poni cura-
vit Anno Dui MDCXXIII
In Hoc tumalo jacet con civ-
em S Valenti Salvina
A Vizenza qua migravit Bo
ecv svb v Mensis

3.

      Sacred
to the memory of
Color Serjeant
Cornelius Sargeson
51 King's Own Light Infantry
who departed this life
the 19th December 1827
aged 34 years
Erected by his brother
non-commissioned officers

4.

Sacred
to the memory of
Captn Woolcombe
90th Light Infantry
who departed this life
Jany 3rd Anno Domini 1829
aged 36 years

5.

Sacred
to the memory
of
Ensign J Sankey
90th Regt Light Infantry
who departed this life
on the 19th Septr 1828
after a short illness
in the 27th year of his age

6.

Sacred
to the memory of
James Cowan, Privt
Soldier 90th Lt Infantry
who dieparted (sic) this life
31st Dec 1828
aged 37 years

7.

Sacred to the memory
of
Sergt George Shaw
38th Regt
who departed this life
27th April 1841
aged 24 years
Erected by his Brother Soldiers as
a mark of respect

8.

Sacred
to the memory of
John Mills, died 14th September [1810?]
John Bates, died 2nd December [1810?]
James Harrison, died 5th May 1811
John Widley, died 24th june 1811
Noah Clark, died 22nd July 1811
Drumr Jas Storey, died 30th July 1811
First Battn, 35th Regt of Foot
Erected by their brother soldiers

9.

Sacred to the memory
of
Mary Hannah Wilson
daughter of J C Wilson, 19th Regt
who departed this life 19th July 1813,
aged 13 months
Suffer little children to come unto me, and
forbid them not, for of such is the Kingdom of God

10.

Sacred
to the memory
of
In---, aged 3 years
A ---

11. [On the east wall, north of the church]

IHS
Sacred
to the memory of
Private Patrick Jorden,
97th Regiment
who departed this life
27th August 1842
aged 22 years
Erected by his comrades

12.
Sacred to
the memory of Gunr & Driver James Green
who departed this life the 5th of July 1831
aged 28 years
My Mother doth for me weep, As I now lie in silent
Sleep, the Sun of God has heard my prayer, I hope in
Heaven to meet her there.
Dear friends, when on my grave you stand, my
Tombstone to read is at your command, do not forget
The blessed day that God above will call you all this way
A comrade, kind friend sincere, a goodhearted Royal
Artillery Man lies buried here
This stone erected by Bombardier Chas King
of Major I Lingley's Company, 7th Bn, R Artillery [Resident of Cerigo]

13.
Sacred
to the memory of
Corporal James Hunt, Vth
Fusiliers who died at
Cerigo on the 19th of July
1840, aged 33 years. Much
regretted by his comrades
There is a joy that ne'er grows dim
A smile that ne'er can leave us.
If we be reconciled to Him
who gave Himself to save us
This tablet is erected at the
Request of the Officers and
Soldiers of the detachment

14.
†
Sacred
to the memory of
Bridget, wife of Sergt Michael
Moffatt, Royal Artillery
who departed this life on
the 30th July 1826
aged 44 years
May she rest in peace
Amen

15.
IHS
Sacred
to the memory of
Private Thomas Casey
97th Regiment
who departed this life
22nd February 1842,
aged 35 years
Erected by his Comrade soldiers
Stand up, my soul, shake off thy fears
And gird the gospel armour on,
March to the gates of endless joy
Where thy great Captain Saviour's gone.

16.
Sacred
to the memory of
Margt McCormick
Daughter of
Gunner P McCormick
RA
who departed this life
30 Augt 1824
aged 7 months

17.
Sacred
to the memory
of
Gunner T Robinson
Royal Artillery
who departed this life
3rd Augt 1824
aged 35 years

18.
Sacred to the memory
of Private Jo^h Kelly
Captn McCrummens' Comp
11th Regt, who died at
St Nicolo on 19th Septer
1834
aged 26 years
This is erected by
His Comrades

19.

Sacred
to the memory of
Private Edward Hackney
51 King's Own Light Infantry
who departed this life
27 February 1827, aged 34 years
Erected to his memory
by his brother soldiers

20.

Sacred
to the memory of Elizabeth
daughter of John and Mary
Roberts of His Majesties 10th Regt
of Infantry who departed this
life the 17th of August 1830,
aged 15 months
The Great Jehovah full of love
An Angel bright did send
To take our little harmless dove
Whose joy shall never end

21.

Sacred
to the memory of
Thos Newman, the infant
son of Corpl and Mrs Newman
R Artillery, who departed this
life 11th Augt 1848, aged 19 days
In this narrow cell I lie
Do not mourn for me or cry
This is the will of our Lord
To live so short in this World

22.

Sacred
to the memory
of
Private Wm Rowland, aged 35 years
E M Homfield, 30 years
M L Curley, 29 years
Of the King's Own Light Infantry
who departed this life AD 1826
Erected by their
brother soldiers

23.

IHS
†
Sacred
to the memory of
Pt Andrew McCarthy, 97 Regt
who departed this life
at Sanniolo the 20th
May AD 1846
aged 29 years
Erected by his comrades

24.

IHS
Sacred
to the memory of
Private Thomas Hearns
97th Regiment
who departed this life
20th of Sept 1812
aged 30 years
Erected by his comrades

25.

Sacred
to the memory of
Corpl Michael McHugh
97th Regt
who died on 14 August 1845

26.

Sacred to the memory of
Private Joseph Fenesty
38th Regiment
who departed this life
10th October 1841
aged 23 years
erected by his comrades

27.
Sacred
to the memory of
Gunr & Driver Rob Carr
of No 4 Coy, 6th Bn, Royal Arty
who died at Cerigo on the
21st May 1846,
aged 41 years

28.
IHS
†
Sacred
to the memory of
Pte W Thompson, 1st Bn 97th Regt
who was killed at Cerigo on the
21st Augt AD 1816, aged 22 years
Here rests his head upon the lap of earth,
A youth to fortune and to fame unknown.
Fair science frowned not on his humble birth,
And melancholy mark'd him for her own.

29.
Sacred to
the memory
of
Cl W Hewitt, Lt Compy
First Battn 26th Regt
Died 8 February
1848
aged 25 years

30. [On south wall of cemetery]

Sacred to the
memory
of
Jern Driscoll, aged 26 yrs
John Nowlan, aged 24 yrs
Patk Dixon, aged 22 yrs
of the
41st Regiment
of
Foot
This stone was erected by the
Officers and men of the Detach[t] as
a token of respect to the memory of
their departed Comrades who were
treacherously murdered at Cerigo
on the 4th April 1852 by exiles
from Zante
Murder!
Murder, most foul as in the best it is.
But this most strange, foul and unnatural

31.

Sacred
to the memory of
Private Evan Richards
HM 41st Regt of Foot
who departed this life on
the 28th May AD 1852
aged 29 years
Erected by his comrades as a mark of respect

31.

Sacred
to
the memory
of
Pt Thos Patterson
31st Regt
died 8th April 1854,
aged 21 years

32.

IHS
Sacred
to
the memory of Pte Michael
Butler, 1st Battn, 9th Regiment
who departed this life on
the 28th of July 1860, aged 21
years and 8 months
This stone was erected by
the Officers and non Commissioned
Officers and men of the above
Battalion as a last token
of Respect to their Deceased
Comrade Soldier
Come, Holy Ghost, Creator, Come
From thy bright heavenly throne.
Come take possession of my soul
and make it all thy own.
Requiescat in pace

33.

To the memory
of
Mary Rennix,
daughter of J Rennix, 31st Reg
who died 12th July 1854, aged
14 months

34. [West wall of cemetery]

Sacred
to the memory
of
Thos Fitzpatrick
son of H Fitzpatrick
90th Lt Iy
who departed this life 24th
Feb 1824, aged 9 months
& 6 days

35.
Sacred
to the memory
of
Augustus Frederick
son of Captain Joseph Richardson
of the 75th British Regiment
who departed this life
on the 8th of November 1820
aged
2 years, 5 months and 15 days

36.
Sacred
to the memory of
James Wright
the son of Sergt Wright, 90th L
who departed this life 17th Aug 1820 (?),
aged 3 (?) months
Ete ...
Death ...
The ...
And bid ...

37. [Under no 36]
IHS
†
Sacred
to the
memory of Private John Riely
of Her Majesty's 7th Regt who departed
this life 31st July 1850, aged 22 years
He was respected by
His Superiors and
beloved by his Comrades

38.
In memory
of Thomas
the son of Michael McEvoy,
late of the 75th Regt
who died 22nd Decr 1820
aged
3 years

39.

†
Sacred
to the memory
of
Amelia Riley, daughter of
P Riley
[rest illegible]

40.

Sacred
to the memory of
Walter Hyde
... of Nov 1823
Weep not for me, my parents dear,
I am not dead but sleeping here.
As I am now as ye must be,
Therefore prepare to follow me.

41.

Sacred
to the memory
of
Lieut Wilm
Hawthornthwaite
35th Regt of Foot
who departed this life
1st March 1810, aged 28 years
Erected by his brother Officers

42.

Sacred
to the memory of
Margaret Edwards
who departed this life
29th Novr
aged 2 yrs, 7 months

43.

Sacred
to the memory of
Hannah, daughter
of Robert (?) and Ann
Evans of ...
Lt Infantry who
departed this
life 29 (?) July (?) 182[0 or 8]
aged 1 year

44.

Sacred
to the memory of
James Richardson Edwards
son of James & Elizabeth Edwards
75th Regt of Foot
who departed this life
31st of October
1820
aged 5 months

45.

Here lies
Edmund
the infant son
of Capt
Edmund Darley
of the 39th
British Regt
1811

46.

IHS
Sacred to
the memory of
Ann Brannan,
Daughter of Sergt Brannan
Private soldier in the .. Regiment
Departed this life the 25th (?)
1818, aged 4 years

In the same grave
with her sister
are placed the remains
of Margaret Brannan
who departed this life
27 Nov 1820
aged 4 years, 7 days
Rests her heart when ...
-wh her parents.
God pleased to call
... this ..
of Cerigo Isle lives ...
... Defaced where I am ...

47.

Sacred
to the memory
of Charlotte
daughter of James and
Catherine McCulloch
of Her Britannic
Majesty's
78th Regt of Foot
who died ... Sepr 1819
aged 10 months

48.

IHS
Sacred to the memory
of
Margaret (?), daughter of
Hugh and Mary Fannon of
the 73rd Regt who departed
this life the 21st Sept 18[2]5
aged 3 (?) years & 9 (?) months
Weep not for me, my parents dear,
I am not dead but sleeping here.
As I am now as ye must be,
Therefore prepare to follow me.

49.
Sacred
to the memory of
Sirenia, daughter of George
Barrow, Private Soldier, 51 KO
LI and Elizabeth, his wife
who departed this life
11th June 1827, aged 1 month and
8 days
The great Jehovah, full of love
An angel bright did sent
To take our little harmless dove
Whose Joy shall never end

50.
Sacred
to the memory
of Rhoda, daughter
of James Hone, Privt
51 KOLI and Frances
His wife who departed
this life – November 1826
aged – months and 12 days
The great Jehovah, full of love
An angel bright did sent
To take our little harmless dove
Whose Joy shall never end

51. [Short wall facing west wall of cemetery]
†
Sacred
to the memory of John and
William Hyde, sons of
Walter and Bridget Hyde
who departed this life
Former on the 19th (?) Octr, aged 10
years and 6 months, the
latter on the 23rd Oct 1824
aged 4 years and 5 months
90th Lt Infantry

52.

Sacred
to the memory of J A Caroll
Son of Sergt P Caroll, 97th Regt
who departed this life on the
25th Feby, aged 3? years,
3 months and five days
Weep not for me, my parents dear,
I am not dead but sleeping here.
As I am now as ye must be,
Therefore prepare to follow me.

53.

Sacred
to
the memory of
Mrs E Speranza, wife
of Dr Speranza, PM
who died at Cherigo
on the 3rd April 1856
aged 33 years

Index

Aberdeen, 4th Earl of, 11
Adam, Frederick, 6
Alexander, Otho, 30
Ansted, David Thomas, 7
Arch, G L, 17
Aspioti, Marie, 7
Atkinson, Margaret, 11

Barnes, John D, 18
Barnes, Robert, 18
Bevan, Dorothy Lydia, 22
Bevan, Leslie Oliver, 22
Bevan, Mary, 22
Bevan, Thomas, 22
Bobou-Stamate, V, 9
Bowen, George Ferguson, 7, 9, 10
Bowman, John S, 8
Briffa, Victor Emmanuel, 22
Brincat, Antonia, 20
Brincat, Carmelo, 20
Brincat, Clothilde, 20
Brincat, Joseph, 20
Brudenell-Bruce, Lord C F, 29
Busson, Cyril, 20
Butler, L, 18
Byron, Lord, 9, 10

Calligus, Eleni, 8
Campbell, James, 6
Capodistrias, John, 9, 19
Chircop, J, 8
Clark, A H, 20
Clark, Frances Emily, 20
Clark, George Alexander, 22
Clark, Hilda Mary, 22
Clark, Jane Elizabeth, 22
Cochran, Peter, 9
Colborne, John, 6
Concina, Ennio, 7
Coupland, Reginald, 8
Crawley, C W, 19
Crossley, George Henry, 22
Crossley, Kenneth, 22
Crossley, Sarah Ann, 22
Crummer, James Henry, 10
Crummer, Katerina Georgia, 10
Crummer, Samuel, 10

D'Istria, Dora, 8
Dakin, Douglas, 19
Dandolo, Antonio, 9

Davie, Michael, 21
Davy, J, 9
Denattista, Antonio, 22
Dixon, Cyril Williams, 8, 9
Dodds, Stan, 21
Dontas, Domna N, 19
Douglas, Howard, 6
Dubin, Marc, 8
Durrell, Lawrence, 9

Eldridge, C C, 8
Ellison, Cyril, 20
Ellison, Edward, 20
Ellison, Mary, 20
Eva, Ellen, 22
Eva, Frederick, 22
Eva, Stanley John, 22

Foss, Arthur, 7
Franklin, John, 10

Gallant, Thomas, 19
Gardiner, Leslie, 21
Gates, Dorothy Mary, 22
Giffard, E, 9
Gilchrist, Hugh, 9
Gill, John, 9
Giraudi, Giovanni, 21
Gladstone, William Ewart, 6
Gordon, Thomas, 19
Granville, George, 8
Gregory, Desmond, 18
Grenville, George Nugent, 6
Grey, Earl, 12
Guilford, Lord, 9
Gulley, Alice M, 20
Gulley, Eliza, 20
Gulley, Lewis Joseph, 20
Gulley, Nathaniel, 20
Gunning, Lucia Patrizio, 8

Hales, Alice, 22
Hales, Gordon Henry, 22
Hales, Gordon Henry (snr), 22
Hall, James, 10
Hannell, David, 8
Harby, Clement, 29
Heppner, Harald, 17
Herbert, Arthur James, 10
Hills, N L, 9
Holding, Norman, 18
Hopwood, John, 12

221

Hoskin, Ernest William, 20
Hoskin, Frances Emily, 20

Jervis-White-Jervis, Henry, 7
Jones, John Arthur, 10

Kaldis, W P, 19
Katsaros, Spiros, 7
Kaufman, David, 18
Keeton, Cyril, 22
Keeton, Frederick, 22
Keeton, Grace, 22
Keeton, Ivy, 22
Kinloch, A, 8
Kirkwall, Viscount, 8
Knott, Dorothy Mary, 22
Knott, Joseph, 22
Knott, Joseph Venning Noel, 22
Knox, Bruce, 8
Kolyv-Karaleka, Marianne, 12

Lambros, Paul, 18
Le Mesurier, Cecil Brooke, 10
Le Mesurier, Nicolina, 10
Lear, Edward, 9
Leggett, Eric, 21
Leonard, Elizabeth, 22
Leonard, Thomas, 22
Leveson Gower, Arthur F G, 30
Lewis, Charles, 20
Lewis, Charles Anthony, 20
Lewis, Maud, 20
Lord, Walter Frewen, 9
Lowry, W, 11

Mackenzie, James Alexander Stewart, 6
Maitland, Thomas, 6, 9
Matton, Raymond, 7
McKenna, George, 22
McKenna, Mary Ellen, 22
Morris, Ronald, 22
Müller, Christian, 9

Napier, Charles James, 9
Nikiforou-Testone, Aliki, 7
Nugent, Lord, 6

Orkney, George 6th Earl, 8
Oswald, - (General), 5
Oswald, John, 11

Palmerston, Lord, 8
Pappas, Nicholas Charles, 18
Parish, Woodbine, 9
Paul, R T, 21
Phillips, Baron John, 21
Phillips, E J, 20

Phillips, Horatio Lloyd, 20
Phillips, Joan, 20
Plessos, Katerina Georgia, 10
Pratt, Michael, 8
Preschel, Pearl Liba, 18
Purcell, Mary, 12

Rodger, N A M, 18
Rogers, John Henry, 20
Routledge, Charles Allison, 20
Routledge, Mary G, 20
Routledge, Robert, 20

Sayers, Emily, 22
Sayers, Eva, 22
Sayers, Ralph, 22
Sayers, William Harry, 22
Schaw, Henry, 11
Schaw, J S, 11
Seaton, Lord, 6, 8, 12
Selby, William H, 21
Seymour, Anthony, 8
Sherrard, Philip, 9
Sinclair, James, 11
Sinclair, James (snr), 11
Spiridione Zancarol, Count, 10
Stamatopoulos, Nondas, 7
Stanbra, E, 20
Stanmore, 1st Baron, 11
Stavrinos, Miranda, 8
Storks, Henry Knight, 6
Sturdza, Mihail Dimitri, 10
Swinnerton, Iain, 18

Thurston, Anne, 12, 18
Tsitsonis, S E, 8
Tumelty, J J, 8

Vaudoncourt, F G de, 9

Ward, Henry George, 6
Warner, C, 20
Warner, E C, 20
Warner, Fred, 20
Watts, Christopher T, 19
Watts, Michael J, 19
Weaver, Agnes N, 22
Weaver, John, 22
Weaver, Peter, 22
Wildy, Ted, 19
Willett, David, 9
Williams, H W, 9
Williamson, W, 20
Willis, George B, 11
Willis, George Henry Smith, 11
Wilson, William, 21

Index 223

Winter, Arthur James, 22
Winter, Brian James, 22
Winter, Winifred Annie, 22
Winterbottom, Sam, 22
Winterbottom, Sam (snr), 22
Winterbottom, Sarah Ann, 22
Wood, Elise, 20
Wood, George, 20
Wood, James, 20

Woodhouse, C M, 19
Wright, Quincy, 22
Wrigley, W David, 8, 9, 18, 19
Wynyard, Edward Buckley, 11
Wynyard, William, 11

Young, John, 6
Young, Martin, 9

Index to Cemetery Inscriptions

This includes the transcripts of the Corfu parish register (on p11-14) and the GRO register of deaths in the Ionian Islands on p15.

A

-, Sarah, 64
Abbott, Esaw, 140
Acco, Jehuddah, 13
Acco, Joseph Samuel, 13
Adair, - (Capt), 54
Adair, Alfred McGregor, 54
Adam, Frederick, 35
Adams, Catherine, 62
Aichinger, Carolina Antonia, 117
Airey, Catherine, 179
Airey, George (Sir), 179
Allan, James, 106
Allan, Robert, 84
Allen, John, 58
Amalis, -, 149
Andain. See Adair
Anderson, James, 107
Anderson, John, 146, 177
Anderson, Mary Jane, 107
Anderson, Robert, 191
Ano, Speranza, 13
Ansell, Augustus E H, 193
Appleby, Thomas, 17
Archer, Andrew, 203
Archer, F B, 118
Archer, Francis Goodrich, 118
Archer, Giovanna, 203
Archer, William, 203
Armour, J, 166
Arrowsmith, Esther, 117
Arrowsmith, James Parrot, 117
Arrowsmith, John William, 117
Artavanis, Constantin, 15

Artavanis, Euridiki, 15
Arter, G, 155
Ash, Thomas, 165
Ashmore, Edward, 82
Ashton, Samuel, 58
Aubrey, Anne Jane, 17
Aubrey, Charlotte, 17
Avouris, Spyros, 12

B

Baillie, Frederick, 51
Baker, Adeline, 79
Baker, Frances, 17, 80
Ball, J, 155
Ballaam, M, 174
Bankaw, George, 84
Barber, James, 90
Bardenfletch, Olin, 128
Barff, Samuel, 204
Barker, Alaric, 137
Barnett, J, 133, 142
Barnett, John William, 15
Barnett, Melia, 15
Barr, Edward Frederick, 127
Barr, Joseph, 79
Barrow, Elisabeth, 88
Barrow, Elizabeth, 219
Barrow, George, 88, 219
Barrow, Sirenia, 219
Barry, Eliza, 68
Barry, Garrett, 68
Barry, John, 68
Baskett, Robert, 106
Bass, Catherine, 157
Bass, William, 97, 157

Bastom, William, 94
Bate, George, 173
Bateman, William, 174
Bates, John, 207
Bavill, J, 155
Beal, George Thomas, 15, 117
Beal, John, 15, 105
Beal, Mary Ann, 105
Beckman, Heinrich C, 15
Begbie, James, 106
Bell, Eliza White, 17
Bell, Robert, 67
Bennett, George, 173
Beresford, G de la Poer, 107
Beresford, Walter Montgomery, 107
Bernard, Augusto, 64
Bernard, Mary, 64
Bernard, Matilda Anne, 64
Berridge, John, 160
Bidwell, Robert, 170
Bingham, Bridget, 47
Bingham, Charlotte Anne, 47
Bingham, Elizabeth, 71
Bingham, Peter, 71
Bingham, William, 47
Bird, James, 171
Bishop, William, 138
Blakaney, Robert, 157
Blakeney, Robert, 158
Blaker, John, 134
Blanckley, Edward J, 123
Bodie, P, 69
Boehmer, Henry William, 98
Bolton-Johnson, William Charlton, 15
Bowdedge, John, 164
Bowden, Robert James, 17
Bowen, Edward George Roma, 113
Bowen, Emma, 112
Bowen, George Ferguson, 113
Bowen, Jane, 112
Bowen, William, 112
Bowyer, Thomas, 134
Boylan, M C, 135
Boylan, Mary Catherine, 135
Boylan, P, 135
Boylan, Patrick William, 135
Boyle, William, 159
Bozard, Thomas, 61
Bradshaw, Elizabeth Jane, 17
Bradshaw, Frederick William, 17
Brandreath, Sarah, 46
Brandreath, Thomas A, 46
Brannan, -, 218
Brannan, Ann, 218

Brannan, Margaret, 218
Bratt, Joseph, 173
Breakwell, Alfred C, 17
Brettel, Moses, 173
Brewer, Harriet, 17
Brewer, Nicholas, 138
Bridge, - (Capt), 124
Bridge, Bernard Cyrian Edward, 124
Bridge, Isabella, 124
Bridge, Winifred Emma Isabella, 124
Brinker, William, 84
Brogden, J, 166
Brogden, T, 155
Brogden, W, 155
Brosman, Patrick, 17
Broughton, Amelia, 16
Broughton, Jane, 17, 191
Broughton, Thomas, 17, 98, 191
Browess, John, 134
Brown, - (Lieut), 53
Brown, Anne Mary, 53
Brown, Arthur, 159
Brown, Charles Henry Crawford, 53
Brown, E, 93
Brown, Edith, 129
Brown, Edward, 94
Brown, Eleanor, 53
Brown, Elisabeth, 87
Brown, Elizabeth, 129
Brown, Emily, 129
Brown, Fred C, 129
Brown, Isaac, 56
Brown, John, 134
Brown, John Carew, 41
Brown, William, 134, 194
Brown, William Abraham, 87
Browne, Laura, 17
Bubina, Eliza Emily, 55
Buchanan, Gilbert John, 112
Buchanan, John, 178
Buchanan, Matilda Mary Ann, 178
Buckley, Daniel, 161
Budding, Hezekiah, 99
Bulgari, Count Cristochilo, 15
Bulgari, Countess Theodora, 15
Burke, J, 133
Burke, Michael, 73
Burns, George, 161
Burns, Maddalena, 156
Burns, Magdalene, 16
Burns, W, 155
Burton, J, 155
Butler, M, 133
Butler, Michael, 214

Index to Cemetery Inscriptions   225

Byers, Richard, 81
Byrne, James, 197
Byrnes, Lawrence, 169
Byrom, Ellen, 141
Byrom, W, 141
Bysooth, Joseph, 134

C

Cachill, Patrick, 70
Cachill, Thomas, 70
Cahill, Mary, 165
Caldwell, James, 173
Callagan, John, 76
Calligary, Esmeralda Harriet, 15
Calligary, Nicole, 15
Calvert, William, 89
Calvin, Sarah, 68
Calvin, Timothy, 68
Came, William, 134
Campatan, Eleonor, 76
Campatan, William, 76
Campbell, Elizabeth, 103
Campbell, Francis, 101, 103
Campbell, J, 119
Campbell, James, 163
Campbell, Margaret, 101, 103
Cannon, Augustine, 173
Caridi, Alexander, 15
Caridi, E, 15
Carling, Thomas, 16
Caroll, J A, 220
Caroll, P, 220
Carpenter, Richard, 174
Carr, Rob, 212
Carrett, Charles, 17
Carry, Thomas, 66
Carter, Abraham, 122
Carter, Ann, 16
Carter, Jane, 123
Carteris, Emma Louisa Ann, 122
Cartwright, John William, 17
Cartwright, William, 48
Carvill, Joseph Thomas, 120
Casey, Thomas, 135, 209
Cavanagh, William, 17
Chadwick, Joseph, 154
Charlton, Robert, 152, 156
Charteris, Eliza, 122
Charteris, Helen, 108
Charteris, W, 108
Charteris, William, 122
Chiaranda, F L, 185

Chiaranda, Sarabella, 188
Ching, Samuel, 167
Chown, Edward, 173
Christian-Deverell, William, 131
Ciles, E, 134
Clancarty, Earl, 121
Claridge, Richard, 84
Claridge, Sarah, 105
Claridge, William, 105
Clark, Ellen Rose, 112
Clark, Frederick Henry, 182
Clark, George Dodd, 186
Clark, James, 36
Clark, Noah, 207
Clark, Patrick, 72
Clark, Robert, 106
Clarke, Richard, 145
Clayton, Alfred Robert, 17
Clayton, Emily Robertina, 17
Clements, C, 155
Clinton, Augusta, 38
Clough, Mary, 60
Clough, Mary (jnr), 60
Clough, Towers, 60
Clunan, Mary, 17
Coaggs, J, 133
Coats, Catherine, 88
Coats, William, 88
Collings, Daniel Stratton, 115
Collings, William, 144
Collins, Edward, 79
Collinson, Joan Frances, 112
Cologan, John Bestard, 74
Cologan, Therese, 74
Coltherts, John Sonol Michael, 164
Conally, Michael, 17
Condi, Demetrio Costa, 15
Condi, Leila Louisa, 15
Connock, Thomas, 115
Connolly, J, 155
Connor, Mary, 77
Connor, Nicolas, 77
Connors, John, 76
Conway, P, 72
Conyngham, George, 54
Conyngham, Olivia Lonon, 54
Cook, Benjamin, 166
Cook, C, 133
Cooke, James, 96
Coombs, Mark, 99
Cooper, I, 95
Cooper, James Mitchell, 95
Cooper, R, 155
Cope, Edward, 16

Cope, Thomas, 90
Cordell, Thomæ, 192
Cortesius, Daloysius, 205
Corvin, Alexander, 148
Coulling, Emily, 14
Coulling, James, 14
Cousins, Thomas, 97
Cove, H R, 145
Coveney, Daniel, 70
Cowan, James, 206
Cox, Charles, 196
Cox, John E, 134
Cozziris, Emily, 121
Craig, F, 183
Craig, Martha, 183
Craigie, David, 42
Craigie, George Clarke, 42
Cramp, Edgar, 151
Crawford, - (Lieut Col), 34
Crawford, Charles Quentin Gregan, 15
Crawford, Charlotte, 34
Crawford, Henry Smart, 34
Crawford, McCoolog, 34
Crawford, Robert G, 15
Creighton, Arthur Onslow, 174
Croggan, Mary, 189
Croggan, S A, 189
Croggan, W O, 189
Cromer, William, 116
Cross, John, 92
Crowley, Catherine, 133
Crowther, G, 155
Crowther, T, 166
Crozier, Susanna S, 116
Crozier, William, 16
Crump, W, 133
Cuddiley, Thomas, 164
Cuming, William, 32
Cummins, William, 85
Cunningham, Jane, 167
Cunningham, Patrick, 167
Cure, T M, 133
Curley, M L, 210
Curtain, M, 133
Cutterson, John, 78

D

D'Everell, William, 16
da Roma, Diamantina, 113
Dabourn, Frederick, 143
Danby, - (Col Sgt), 143
Danby, Elisabeth, 143

Danby, Ellen, 143
Danby, Emma, 143
Daniel, Charles, 196
Daniel, Ellenor, 196
Darley, Edmund (jnr), 217
Darley, Edmund (snr), 217
Darrah, -, 176
Darrah, George William F, 176
Darral, Patrick John, 156
Davies, John, 49
Davies, Mary, 49
Davies, N, 134
Davies, Thomas, 15
Davis, Caroline Kircudbright, 91
Davis, Charles, 175
Davis, H I, 63
Dawkins, Francis Henry, 38
Dawkins, Henry, 38
Dawson, Arthur Edwin, 174
Dawson, Stephen, 183
Day, Henry, 142
Day, William, 66
de Cornory, Antonio, 132
de Norman, Emma, 126
de Norman, Grace Ellen, 13
de Norman, Harriett, 13
de Norman, John, 13, 126
Dedrick, Frederick, 197
Deer, Thomas, 173
Devannaoh, Jeremiah, 173
Deverell, Eleonor, 156
Deverell, William, 156
Dickens, Frederick, 158
Dicks, Brian, 7
Dillon, Alfred, 162
Dillon, Mary, 162
Dix, Daniel, 173
Dixon, Cecilia Peorina, 117
Dixon, Patrick, 213
Dixon, William, 117
Dodsworth, Alexander, 182
Donnellan, Michael, 154
Donolan, J, 133
Donolan, M, 133
Donting, M, 198
Donting, M A, 198
Doolon, Michael, 174
Dores, Henry, 111
Doser, Amelia, 14
Doser, Joseph, 14
Doudie, David, 178
Doudie, Elizabeth, 178
Douglas, Howard (Sir), 38
Douglas, Lady, 38

Index to Cemetery Inscriptions

Douglas, Sarah Mary Harcourt, 38
Dowling, W, 133
Dowling, William, 169
Downey, Elisabeth Margaret, 130
Downey, M, 130
Downing, Urb, 67
Doyly, G, 162
Driscoll, Jern, 213
Dugan, John, 63
Durban, Thomas, 147
Dyart, Henry, 168
Dyz, John, 153

E

Earle, Arthur Maxwell, 118
Earnshaw, Ellen, 154
Earnshaw, J, 154
Earnshaw, James, 154
Earwaker, John, 84
East, W, 139
Eddiken, John, 95
Edwards, Elizabeth, 217
Edwards, James, 162, 217
Edwards, James Richardson, 217
Edwards, Joseph Dawson, 138
Edwards, Margaret, 216
Elderhost. *See* Elenhurst
Elect, John, 134
Elefebure, Henry Leopold Elic, 126
Elenhurst, - (Col), 125
Elenhurst, Charles Robert, 125
Elenhurst, Frances, 125
Ellicombe, Charles Ford, 46
Ellicombe, George Bradford, 46
Ellicombe, Geraldine Frances D'Aguildar, 46
Elliott, James, 140
Elliott, Mary Elisabeth, 140
Elliott, William Andrew, 172
Elmer, H, 155
Epwartby, William D, 138
Evans, Ann, 217
Evans, H, 133
Evans, Hannah, 217
Evans, James, 173
Evans, Robert, 217
Evelyn, Gertrude, 16

F

Fairey, Charles, 66

Fairfoot, H Robert Dudley, 102
Fairfoot, Robert, 102
Fanenan, F, 53
Fanenan, Susanna Maria Wilhelmina, 53
Fannon, Hugh, 218
Fannon, Margaret, 218
Fannon, Mary, 218
Fanquier, Charles, 100
Fanquier, Corinn, 101
Fattnald, - (Capt), 110
Fattnald, Eliza Hay, 110
Fels, Bertha, 132
Fels, Eliza, 108
Fels, Martin, 132
Fels, Oswald, 131
Fels, Thomas, 132
Fenesty, Joseph, 211
Ferguson, H A, 109
Ferguson, John, 191
Ferguson, William, 84
Fielding, W, 110
Fisher, Thomas, 99
Fitzpatrick, H, 214
Fitzpatrick, Thomas, 214
Fix, John, 134
Flack, Caroline, 37
Flack, Eliza, 13
Flack, Eliza Weale, 37
Flack, John, 37, 40
Flack, John William, 38
Flack, Joseph I B C, 111
Flack, Martha, 122
Flack, Susanna H, 40
Flack, Susannah, 37
Flack, Thomas, 122
Fletcher, William, 14
Fletcher, William Bainbridge, 14
Foley, J, 201
Folvery, Alexius, 132
Foote, William, 202
Forbes, Robert, 33
Ford, - (Gen), 108
Ford, Walter William, 174
Forrest, Anne, 15
Forrest, Caroline Amelia, 52
Forrest, George, 118
Forrest, James, 118
Forrest, R W, 118
Forrest, Robert, 52
Forrest, Robert William, 15
Foster, Elizabeth, 114
Foster, J, 155
Foster, Thomas William, 114
Fox, -, 179

Fox, John, 145
Foy, Isabella, 103
Foy, William Henry, 103
Freeman, I, 110
Freer, William Gardner, 32
Frey, Amalie, 149
Frey, Amelia, 14
Frey, Ernest, 149
Frey, Johanna Magdalena, 149
Frey, Johanna Magdalina, 14
Frey, Johannes, 14, 149
Frey, John, 14
Frey, Richard, 149
Frey, Ulright, 14
Frey, Wilhelm, 149
Frost, Catherine, 149
Frost, Georgina, 149
Frost, J, 135
Frost, William, 149
Fudler, Robert, 98
Fuller, Thomas, 140
Fyers, Thomas, 121
Fyers, Thomas (snr), 121
Fyers, William, 121

G

Gaertner, Babette, 148
Gage, Edward Thomas, 110
Gains, Ernest Trest, 126
Gains, G E, 126
Gall, Hermann, 193
Galloway, William, 174
Galway, Viscount, 36
Gander, Francis, 141
Ganderton, J, 133
Gant, James, 70
Gant, William, 70
Gardiner, George R, 116
Gardiner, Henry Thomas, 116
Gardiner, Mary Anne, 116
Garland, Thomas, 67
Gaskeath, Thomas Walter, 105
Gay, -, 120
Gay, Ada, 120
Gay, Frances Mary, 120
George, Thomas, 97
German, William, 152
Gibbons, Henry, 91
Gibbons, Lucy Eliza, 91
Gibbs, J, 90
Gibson, Alexander Frances Ogilvie, 67
Gibson, T, 155

Gibson, Thomas, 67
Gifford, George William, 120
Gilchrist, Hugh, 113
Gilchrist, James, 162
Gilchrist, Jane, 162
Gile, - (Col Sgt), 155
Gillegan, John Charles, 74
Gilpin, Arthur, 65
Gilpin, Edward William, 65
Goodall, James, 80
Goodridge, George Thomas, 15
Goodridge, Henry Painter, 15
Goodrunn, William, 16
Gould, W, 133
Grace, William, 80
Grady, Catherine, 75
Grady, Thomas, 75
Graham, Esther, 145
Graham, James, 134
Graham, Joseph, 145
Graham, Margaret Harriet, 104
Graham, Mary, 154
Graham, Susan Ford, 104
Graney, John, 199
Grant, Colquhoun, 184
Grant, Thomas, 129
Grantham, Thomas, 168
Gray, Edward George, 180
Gray, Jane Bertram, 180
Gray, Thomas, 180
Green, G, 133
Green, James, 208
Greenwood, Thomas, 109
Gregory, William, 94
Griffin, David, 141
Grocott, George, 173
Groves, Catherine, 16
Gruby, Edwin, 134
Gubbins, - (Lieut Col), 182
Guibert, Joanne Henriette Phillipine, 16
Guttridge, William, 197
Guy, Thomas, 174
Gysi, Frederick, 131

H

Hacket, R, 55
Hacket, William, 54
Hackney, Edward, 210
Haifron, Robert, 174
Hale, H, 166
Hall, C, 79
Hall, Harriet, 79

Index to Cemetery Inscriptions 229

Hall, James, 66
Hamer, William, 81
Hamilton, Benjamin Usher, 91
Hammick, Elizabeth, 71
Hammick, John, 71
Hammick, John (jnr), 71
Hancock, Caroline, 14
Hancock, Edward, 14
Hancock, Joseph, 82
Hancock, Katherine Irene, 14
Hand, H, 155
Hanly, John, 154
Harby, Clement, 179
Hardy, John, 69
Hardy, Mary, 69
Hardy, Mary (jnr), 69
Hargrave, George, 66
Harley, Alice, 119
Harley, E, 110
Harley, John, 119
Harpwood, Stephen Edmonds, 160
Harries, James, 95
Harris, Elizabeth, 61
Harris, Frances, 61
Harris, Henry Thomas, 181
Harris, John, 61
Harrison, James, 207
Hart, John, 73
Hart, Thomas, 61
Hartell, William, 172
Hartman, August, 15
Hartman, Ernest Frederick, 15
Hartshorn, Samuel, 173
Harvey, Anne, 102
Harvey, Francis Ershire, 151
Harvey, Jane, 102
Harvey, John, 190
Harvey, Thomas, 177
Harvey, William, 102
Haselmere, Emma Maria, 13
Haselmere, John Hartley, 13
Haselmere, Joseph, 13
Hassard, John, 43
Hassard, Susannah, 43
Hassard, Susannah (jnr), 43
Hatherley, James, 16
Hatherly, James, 148
Hatton, Charles, 123
Hawes, Benjamin, 172
Hawthornthwaite, William, 216
Hayes, Edward, 203
Hayes, William, 201
Hayward, Samuel, 184
Hearns, Thomas, 211

Heath, George, 100
Hegarty, M, 155
Hegett, Richard Henry, 94
Heimpel, Elwina, 132
Heimpel, Robert, 132
Henderson, William, 106
Henley, J, 155
Henry, John, 199
Henry, M, 130
Henry, Mary Hannah Jane, 130
Henry, T, 130
Herapaith, William, 101
Herring, George, 95
Hewitt, W, 212
Hewson, Ellen, 78
Hewson, Michael, 78
Hickman, Henry, 49
Hickman, Mary, 49
Hickson, Eliza, 60
Hickson, James, 60
Hickson, Mary, 60
Hickson, William, 60
Hight, W, 155
Hill, -, 194
Hill, Arthur, 15
Hill, Arthur Ernest, 186
Hill, George, 173
Hill, Hanora, 194
Hill, Henry, 175
Hill, John, 15
Hill, Maria Jane, 186
Hill, R F, 186
Hill, Richard Fred, 175
Hill, Richard Thomas, 194
Hillier, J, 133
Hines, Robert, 15
Hoffman, Babette, 16, 147
Hogan, D, 155
Hogan, Daniel, 199
Holder, Elizabeth Henriette, 88
Holder, William, 88
Hollams, John, 126
Homer, J, 133
Homfield, E M, 210
Hone, Frances, 219
Hone, James, 219
Hone, Rhoda, 219
Horne, James, 101
Horne, Margaret, 101
Horne, Moses, 101
Horton, C, 135
Hossack, John, 81
Howse, Charles, 33
Hucker, John, 134

Huddleston, John, 175
Hudson, R, 155
Hughes, -, 70
Hughes, Christine Adrianne Sidney, 14
Hughes, Gladys Carlisle Conway, 16
Hughes, Gladys Zoe Carlisle, 127
Hughes, J W Conway, 127
Hughes, James, 71
Hughes, John W C, 14
Hughes, Owen, 202
Hull, John Trevor, 53
Hull, Thomas A, 10
Hunt, James, 208
Hunt, Michael, 197
Hurley, William, 71
Hurst, Clara, 95
Hurst, E P, 95
Hutton, George F, 173
Hyde, Bridget, 219
Hyde, John, 219
Hyde, Walter, 216, 219
Hyde, William, 219

I

Ibbetson, Denzil, 55
Ibbetson, Fred H, 55
Ibbetson, Martha, 55
Incaman, Joseph Phillips, 151
Irby, Adelaide P, 125
Ives, James, 174

J

Jackson, Ellen B, 141
James, W, 139
Jameson, Elizabeth, 60
Jameson, Henry Percy Mackenzie, 91
Jameson, James, 131
Jameson, Josephine, 91
Jameson, Maria, 91
Jameson, Mary, 91
Jameson, Thomas, 91
Jameson, William, 91
Jarvis, George, 111
Jarvis, Grace, 111
Jarvis, Henry, 111
Jarvis, Rachel Eliza, 111
Jarvis, William, 111
Jeffery, Eliza, 144
Jeffery, R, 144
Jeffs, J, 174

Jeffs, Sarah, 174
Jelicoon, - (Lieut), 51
Jenkins, -, 135
Jenkins, David, 58
Jenkins, David (jnr), 58
Jenkins, James, 151
Johnson, Edward, 43
Johnson, George, 15
Johnston, Catherine, 128
Johnston, George, 62
Johnston, Robert, 128
Johnstone, George, 36
Jones, Edward Charles, 153
Jones, R C, 136
Jones, Richard, 134
Jones, Richard Quigley, 136
Jorden, Patrick, 207

K

Kane, Anthony John, 180
Kane, Benjamin, 180
Kane, Caroline, 180
Keating, I, 57
Keightley, - (Lieut Col), 35, 161
Keightley, Anna, 35
Keightley, Anne, 35, 161
Kekewich, Arthur, 106
Kekewich, Lewis, 106
Kekewich, Samuel Trehawke, 106
Kellock, Adam, 88
Kelly, Joseph, 209
Kemmingham, Patrick, 172
Kemp, Joseph, 190
Kempe, J, 155
Kennedy, J, 155
Kerr, John William Robert, 35
Kerr, Schomberg Robert, 35
Kerrigan, Sarah, 201
Kerrigan, W, 201
Kettlewell, John, 36
Keyt, - (Lieut Col), 51
Keyt, Emilie Lanpetta Powell, 51
Kind, Esther, 121
Kind, Jane, 56
Kind, Sarah, 56
Kind, Thomas, 56
Kind, Thomas William, 56
Kind, William, 121
King, Charles, 208
King, Elizabeth, 83
King, Fanny Maria, 83
King, John, 83

Index to Cemetery Inscriptions

Kirby, Ellen, 181
Kirby, Frances Eliza, 181
Kirby, William, 181
Klingenberg, Nicolays, 31
Kloctzscker, G R Emil, 149
Kluppel, Balthasagar Joseph, 15
Kluppel, Charles George John, 15
Knocker, Mercy, 16, 126
Knocker, Thomas, 126

L

Lambert, George, 84
Lamond, Peter, 31
Landstaff, T, 133
Laseter, Elias, 57
Lauder, Mary, 46
Lawrence, Alfred Macdonald, 45
Lawrence, Samuel Hill, 45
Lazaretto, -, 34
Le Poer Trench, Robert, 16, 121
Leader, George, 95
Leahy, -, 85
Lecazza, Olivia, 183
Lee, James, 90
Lee, Mary Ann, 90
Leech, William, 134
Leflufy, Heddel, 153
Legazza, John, 188
Legazza, Olivia Lee, 188
Leighton, Christine Beveridge, 203
Leighton, David, 203
Lennox, Francis, 89
Leonard, John Brydge, 48
Leonard, Mary Sofia, 48
Lewis, James, 174
Lewis, W, 122
Liebreith, - (Qmr Sjt), 77
Liebreith, Margaret, 77
Liebreith, Martha Louisa, 77
Lindsay, Walter, 84
Lindsey, Annie, 185
Lindsey, Eliza, 185
Lindsey, John, 185, 204
Lindsey, John M, 175
Lindsy, Jeanette, 175
Lingard, L, 155
Lingley, I, 208
Lisle, Robert, 42
Lloyd, Richard C, 161
Lloyd, Samuel, 173
Lockwood, Charles, 137
Lockwood, J, 137

Logan, James, 78
Longstaff, Ann, 123
Longstands, R, 133
Lothian, Marquess of, 35
Loundes, Elizabeth, 189
Loundes, Isaac, 189
Loundes, John W, 189
Loundes, Mary H, 189
Lountzel, Maria Katherine, 192
Loverdo, Dionysius C, 193
Lowdes, Richard F, 138
Lowry, Robert William, 11
Lucton, George, 66
Ludeman, Jean, 153
Lund, Edward, 167
Lyons, William, 134, 145
Lytton, Ernest, 129

M

MacArley, -, 136
MacArley, Harry Arthur, 136
MacArley, William, 136
Macdonald, Donald, 169
Macdonald, Peter J, 45
Maces, Joseph, 134
Mackenzie, Eliza, 131
MacKinlay, - (Col Serjt), 81
MacKinlay, Elizabeth, 81
MacKinlay, John, 81
MacKinlay, Mary Anne, 81
Mackintosh, Alice Telford, 111
Mackintosh, Ellen, 111
Mackintosh, William, 111
Macropoulos, Demetrius, 14
Macropoulos, George, 14
MacSweeney, Michael C M, 75
MacSweeney, Theresa, 75
Mahaffey, James, 134
Manetta, - (Mrs), 130
Manetta, Amelia, 16
Mangan, J, 155
Mariner, Emily, 14
Mariner, James, 14
Marriott, - (Capt), 115
Marriott, Thomas F R, 115
Marsh, Francis, 187
Marsh, Isabella, 187
Marshall, Caterina, 66
Marshall, Charles, 152
Marshall, David, 58
Marshall, George, 66
Marshall, Joseph, 66

Martin, R, 104
Martin, Sarah, 180
Martindale, Benhay, 107
Martindale, Mary Elisabeth, 107
Martindale, Mary Sophia Harriet, 107
Maskell, I J William, 158
Maslin, James, 115
Masterton, John, 61
Matthews, - (Lieut), 35
Matthews, Maria, 190
Mavin, Elizabeth, 77
Mavin, Sarah Anne, 77
Mavin, William, 77
Mayne, Charles, 134
McAllister, Arch, 173
McArley, Emma, 136
McAvoy, Mary Ann, 168
McAvoy, Patrick Louis, 168
McCabe, Owen, 76
McCallum, John, 57
McCammon, John, 175
McCammon, Thomas, 175
McCarthy, Andrew, 211
McCormick, Margaret, 209
McCormick, P, 209
McCrummens, -, 209
McCulloch, Catherine, 218
McCulloch, Charlotte, 218
McCulloch, James, 218
McDonald, Anne, 70
McDonald, James, 70
McDonald, John, 169
McDonald, Mary Ann, 70
McElligot, J, 133
McEvoy, Michael, 215
McEvoy, Thomas, 215
McFarlane, Duncan, 142
McFarlane, William, 106
McGineley, John, 70
McHugh, Michael, 211
McJarlin, James, 66
McKilay, John, 95
McLain, John, 83
McLain, John Edward, 83
McLain, Lydis, 83
McLeod, Jane, 93
McLeod, William, 93
McMahon, - (Dr), 16
McMahon, William, 119
McNiel, Luke, 78
McPherson, - (Lieut), 39
McPherson, M, 39
McPherson, P John, 100
McRoberts, Thomas, 81

Meadows, William George, 160
Mears, R C, 87
Mellor, James, 173
Mennice, Mark Ann, 65
Menzel, Alfred, 153
Merriman, William, 84
Miall, Charles William, 145
Miall, Isabella, 145
Miall, J, 145
Miles, Ann, 187
Miles, Francis, 187
Miles, George, 187
Miller, James, 143
Mills, Edward, 66
Mills, John, 207
Mitchell, Adam, 134
Mitchell, J, 155
Mitchell, Robert, 202
Mitchell, Thomas, 62
Mitchison, Alfred Buckton, 51
Mitchison, Thomas R, 51
Moffatt, Bridget, 208
Moffatt, Michael, 208
Molloy, William, 72
Monckton, Charles Gustavus, 36
Moore, Andrew William, 161
Moore, Charles, 143
Moore, Daniel, 183
Moran, Elizabeth, 200
Moran, John, 173
Moran, M, 155
Moran, Nicholas, 200
Morgan, George, 174
Morgan, Samuel, 173
Morgan, Thomas, 173, 174
Morrison, Joseph, 160
Moss, Elizabeth, 195
Moss, Richard, 195
Moss, Richard William, 195
Mudd, James, 174
Muir Mackenzie, William Pitt, 125
Munro, Donald, 37
Munroe, Hector, 181
Murphy, Frederick, 129
Murray, Mary, 80
Murrey, Mary, 77
Muspratt, Henry, 80
Muspratt, Mary, 80

N

Newall, Ann, 99
Newall, Thomas, 99

Index to Cemetery Inscriptions

Newall, Thomas Phillip, 99
Newman, -, 210
Newman, Thomas, 210
Newton, W J E, 126
Nicholls, George, 15
Nicholls, James, 174
Niel, Edward, 153
Norman, John Lewis, 104
Nowlan, James, 75
Nowlan, John, 75, 213
Numan, Anne Agnes, 68
Numan, Elizabeth, 68
Numan, John, 68

O

O'Callanghan, - (Col Sgt), 155
O'Connor, James, 200
O'Leary, Patrick, 164
O'Reilly, B, 55
O'Reilly, John Frederick, 55
O'Reilly, Louisa Maria, 55
Odgers, James, 95
Ogle, Henry, 42
Organ, Henry, 114

P

Pace, Thomas, 158
Page, Alexander Wilhelm, 13
Page, Alexandra Adelaide, 13
Page, Alice Caroline, 137
Page, Anna, 64
Page, Charlotte, 117
Page, Edward Thomas, 13, 14
Page, Ellen Esther, 64
Page, Emma, 13, 14
Page, Eugine, 64
Page, Frances, 137
Page, Francis Woodley, 13
Page, Fredk William, 137
Page, Gertrude Everin, 121
Page, Henrietta Esther, 13
Page, Ida Annie, 14, 16
Page, Ina Annie, 121
Page, Leopold Dorset, 14
Page, Mathew John, 13, 117
Page, Matthew, 64
Page, Matthew John, 13, 14, 16
Page, Susannah Emily, 13, 14
Page, Victor Louis, 14
Page, Walter Thomas, 14

Papaviero, Julia, 153
Parker, Kate, 16
Parker, W, 133
Parnell, Sylvia Olivia Narcissa Catherine, 193
Parnell, Thomas, 183
Parnell, Thomas Lee, 193
Parsons, Ann Charlotte, 45
Parsons, John Hile, 41
Parsons, John Whitehill, 45
Parsons, Mary Elisabeth, 45
Paterson, - (Rev), 108
Paterson, John, 87
Patterson, Thomas, 213
Paul, David, 188
Paul, James, 182, 188
Pearson, James, 98
Peat, Thomas, 15
Pecco, Christopher, 52
Pecco, Harriet Browne, 52
Penny, William E, 152
Pepporall, William Henry, 63
Perry, Thomas, 134
Peters, John, 141, 145
Petters, John, 134
Petty, William, 41
Pigot, George, 49
Pimlott, Richard, 92
Pitman, Jane, 195
Pitman, Joseph, 195
Pitsey, Wee, 49
Pixton, J, 155
Pollen, James, 112
Portlock, - (Major), 54
Portlock, Harriet, 54
Potter, - (Lieut Col), 34
Potter, Georgina, 34
Potter, John, 95
Powell, Frances Matilda, 116
Powell, J C, 116
Prascodima, - (Mrs), 128
Probyn, - (Governor), 35
Probyn, Edward, 35
Probyn, George, 35
Purdell, Edward, 78
Putton, Robert, 139

Q

Qualermani, Angolina, 15
Quanley, Joseph, 72
Quanley, Thomas S, 72
Quinland, Charles, 13, 59

Quinland, Edith Alice, 13
Quinland, Eliza Flack, 13
Quinland, Elizabeth, 59
Quinland, James, 127
Quinland, Marianne Helen, 13
Quinland, Wilhelmina, 59
Quinland, Wilhelmina Elizabeth Henrietta, 13, 15

R

Rabling, Henry, 65
Rafferty, George, 72
Rafferty, Owen, 72
Rainy, George Hogarth, 16
Raisey, Thomas, 115
Ramsay, - (Comm Gen), 44
Ramsay, Thomas Rattray Blair, 44
Ray, Albert S, 134
Raymond, Ellen Victoria Barry, 130
Raymond, George, 130
Reade, Elisabeth, 111
Reade, Henry Cooper, 111
Reade, Henry Loftus, 111
Reardan, Denis, 200
Reardan, Jeremiah, 200
Reardaut, Jeremiah, 165
Reardaut, Mary, 165
Reid, Catherine, 74
Reid, Eliza, 103
Reid, Ellen, 103
Reid, Helen, 103
Reid, I W, 74
Reid, Robert, 15, 103, 146
Reid, Robert (jnr), 49
Reid, Robert (snr), 49
Rennie, Faith, 142
Rennie, O, 142
Rennix, J, 214
Rennix, Mary, 214
Rewes, William, 67
Rey, John, 185
Richards, Evan, 213
Richardson, Augustus Frederick, 215
Richardson, Joseph, 215
Rickards, N, 110
Riely, John, 215
Riley, Amelia, 216
Riley, P, 216
Roach, M, 133
Roberts, Edward, 86
Roberts, Elizabeth, 210
Roberts, George (jnr), 194

Roberts, George (snr), 194
Roberts, Henry John, 162
Roberts, Isabella Hamat, 195
Roberts, Jacob, 86
Roberts, Jemima, 86
Roberts, John, 162, 210
Roberts, Jon, 195
Roberts, Letitia, 195
Roberts, Mary, 16, 194, 210
Roberts, Richard William, 195
Robertson, - (Lieut Col), 125
Robertson, David, 85
Robertson, Heston Matilda, 125
Robertson, James Frances, 125
Robinson, Denis, 84
Robinson, T, 209
Roche, T, 155
Rooney, - (Serjt), 74
Rooney, Margaret, 74
Roscoe, Thomas, 168
Ross, David, 100
Ross, J, 62
Ross, James, 106
Ross, Mary, 62
Roster, James, 134
Rowland, Denis, 191
Rowland, William, 210
Rudge, William, 96
Rutherford, John, 85
Ryan, Edward, 141
Rycroft, Edward, 104
Rycroft, W J, 104
Rycroft, William, 104
Ryder, George, 174

S

Sabine Browne, Compton, 92
Sabine Browne, Henry, 92
Salter, David, 83
Salter, Elizabeth, 13
Salter, George Piggott, 13
Salter, Sidney Arthur, 13
Sandelis, John, 139
Sandham, Charles, 31
Sandham, William Edward, 31
Sankey, J, 206
Sargeson, Cornelius, 205
Sargint, Catherine Mary, 203
Sargint, Clara, 203
Sargint, Richard, 203
Sargint, Robert Bachelor, 192
Saruchi, John, 113

Saruchi, Mary Ann Elden, 113
Satchfield, J, 133
Saunders, Mary, 177
Savage, Thomas, 134
Scanlon, John, 159
Scargill, - (Major), 39
Scargill, Nathaniel, 39
Scobell, H Harris, 43
Scott, J, 89
Scott, Ricardus Edmundus, 44
Seahan, Caroline, 148
Seahan, Ellen Elisabeth, 148
Seahan, Thomas, 148
Seall, C, 134
Sebright, Charles, 125
Sebright, Georgina Mary Lady, 16
Sebright, Lady, 125
Seelton, P, 155
Shankey, J, 133
Shaw, George, 206
Shea, T, 155
Shea, Thomas, 199
Sheard, Samuel, 64
Shepherd, William, 109
Sheppard, Eleanor, 63
Shiell, William, 98
Shilitoe, George, 141
Shillington, E, 142
Shillington, Fanny, 142
Shilton, P Patrick, 154
Shimmons, William, 174
Shinners, James, 78
Shipton, Dennis, 134
Short, Ada Ellen, 202
Simpson, C, 136
Simpson, E H, 136
Simpson, George, 173
Simpson, John, 84, 184
Simpson, Mary Ellen Edith, 136
Skinner, William, 82
Slackyard, William, 199
Small, Alexander, 86
Smith, Frederick, 73
Smith, Haviland, 47
Smith, Jane, 92
Smith, John, 134, 193, 205
Smith, Margaret, 73
Smith, Robert, 86
Smith, Thomas, 152
Smith, William, 92, 140
Snell, Edward, 177
Soar, S, 155
Soper, Henry, 62
Soper, John William, 39

Soper, N, 39
Soper, Nicolas, 40
Soper, Sarah, 39
Sparkes, George, 176
Spence, George, 84
Spence, John, 170
Spence, John Hercules, 170
Spencer, Oswald, 144
Spenglin, Elwina, 131
Spenglin, G, 132
Spenglin, Gertrude, 131
Spenglin, Gustav, 131
Speranza, - (Dr), 220
Speranza, E, 220
Spittle, Arthur, 152
Stainton, Josh, 65
Stanckyard, W, 155
Stanyard, D, 155, 166
Stapleton, Franck, 139
Steatham, Caroline, 144
Stephens, Edward, 46
Stevens, Alfred, 158
Stevens, George, 204
Stevens, R C M, 204
Steward, Donald, 65
Stewart, Henry, 156
Stewart, William, 106
Storey, James, 207
Stretch, John, 13, 128
Stretch, John Henry, 13
Stretch, Rosine, 13
Stretch, Sophia, 13
Stuart, Alexander, 40
Sullivan, Elizabeth, 198
Summerfield, Charles, 174
Surcumbe, William, 109
Sutton, G P, 16
Sutton, George Pigott, 124
Sutton, William, 124
Swaffield, Alex, 136
Swaffield, F C, 136
Swaffield, J, 136
Swaffield, Martha Caroline, 136
Swaine, J, 108
Swaine, Mary Jane, 108
Swann, Adelaide, 77
Swann, Edward, 119
Swann, Francis John, 77
Swann, Hannah Maxwell, 119
Swann, John, 77
Swann, Louisa, 77
Swann, William, 119

T

Talbot, Catherine, 179
Talbot, Richard, 179
Tarring, William, 146
Taylor, Frederick G, 60
Taylor, Henrietta M, 60
Taylor, James, 59
Taylor, James William, 116
Taylor, John, 186
Taylor, Margaret, 59
Taylor, Mary Quinland, 59
Taylor, Thomas, 120
Taylor, William, 95
Tennent, James, 187
Tharding, Louisa Helen, 118
Tharding, William, 118
Thomas, - (Sgt), 144
Thomas, Charles S, 180
Thomas, Isabella Mary Anne Bertie, 48
Thomas, J, 133
Thomas, Joseph, 179
Thomas, Margaret Emma, 179
Thomas, Mary, 179, 180
Thomas, Patrick Stuart, 180
Thomas, William Frances, 48
Thompson, John, 123
Thompson, W, 212
Thomson, I E, 56
Thomson, James, 67
Thunder, Edward, 151
Toole, Allig Peter, 177
Toole, Anne A, 177
Toole, E A, 176
Toole, Eliza, 175
Toole, Eman, 175
Toole, Emmanuel J C, 175
Toole, Ernest, 15
Toole, Evanthira, 15
Toole, George A, 177
Toole, George Aug, 176
Toole, James, 176
Toole, John Aug, 176
Toole, John Aug jnr, 176
Toole, Marietta, 176
Toole, Marietta J, 177
Toole, Mary L E, 175
Toole, William Anthony, 177
Townsend, - (Co Adjt), 50
Townsend, Jane Maria Theresa, 50
Travers, William, 84
Trigance, - (Assistant Staff Surgeon), 44
Trigance, Louisa Jane, 44

Trisley, E, 155
Trussell, -, 135
Tuckey, C F, 170
Tuckey, Charles Johnly Acht, 170
Tully, John Michael, 135
Tully, Mary Ann, 135
Tully, Michael Frederick, 135
Tully, T, 135
Tully, Thomas, 135
Tunnutt, James, 96
Tuthill, G A, 178
Tyers, William, 160

U

Uniake, Eleonor R, 54
Unwin, Eliza, 197

V

Vachain, Mary, 16
Valsamari, Penelope, 128
Vernon, H A, 120
Vernon, Henry, 158, 187
Vernon, Sophia, 187
Vicars, E, 29
Vince, Catherine, 155
Vince, George, 155
Vince, John, 155
Vise, Victoria, 15
von Kruedener, Arthur, 113
von Lindan, George Helmensdoffer, 113
von Wimmar, Frederick, 157

W

Wadey, James, 95
Wadey, Mercy, 95
Walker, Oliver, 101
Wallace, William, 84
Walman, Emily Ann, 79
Walman, Thomas, 79
Walpole, William, 108
Walsh, Elisabeth, 104
Ward, Patrick, 69
Ward, William, 16, 147
Ware, Charles, 112
Ware, George Henry, 112
Wartman, Jakob, 132
Wasey, W C, 63
Wasey, Willoughby Clement, 67

Index to Cemetery Inscriptions

Watkins, William, 134, 145
Watson, John, 93
Watson, S, 133
Watts, Francis, 89
Weagan, Thomas, 56
Weagar, Catherine, 61
Weagar, Thomas, 61
Weale, Richard, 16, 148
Weale, William, 16, 89, 147
Webber, George, 57
Webber, Henry, 100
Webby, H, 155
Weir, George, 196
Weir, Helen Louisa, 33
Weir, John, 196
Weir, Sara Jane, 196
Weir, Sarah, 196
Welby, George, 199
Wells, Robert, 104
Welsh, Conman, 173
Wentworth, D'Arcy, 133
Wentworth, Sarah, 133
Wentworth, William C, 133
West, Arthur Thomas, 14
West, Emily, 14, 109
West, Frederick, 14
West, John, 109
West, Susan Amelia, 109
Westacott, Annie, 137
Westacott, M, 137
Westacott, M A, 137
Westacott, Martha Elizabeth, 137
Wheat, John, 171
Wheat, John Thomas, 171
Wheat, Joyce, 171
White, Robert, 73
White, Thomas B, 190
Whitfield, Edith Maud, 13, 150
Whitfield, Frances Helen, 15
Whitfield, James, 13, 29
Whitfield, James Fraser, 15
Whitfield, Sarah, 13
Whitmore, J L, 111
Whitney, Luke, 181
Wickendem, Alfred, 143
Widley, John, 207
Wild, John, 63
Wilkin, Ann Charlotte, 150
Wilkin, Anne Charlotte, 14, 16
Wilkin, Emily, 13, 14, 150
Wilkin, Ida Jane Caroline, 13
Wilkin, John, 13, 14, 150
Wilkin, Joseph, 14
Wilkin, Marianne Helen, 14, 16, 150

Wilkinson, I F, 159
Williams, B, 133
Williams, John, 134, 145
Williams, Richard, 57
Williams, Robert, 95
Williams, Thomas, 150
Williamson, J, 133
Williontan, Alexander Zillatoff, 137
Wilson, - (Capt), 96
Wilson, Catherine, 102
Wilson, J C, 207
Wilson, James, 67, 102
Wilson, Louisa, 102
Wilson, Margaret, 102
Wilson, Mary Hannah, 207
Wilson, Samuel, 84
Wilson, William, 94, 102
Winn, Anne Osborne, 124
Winn, George, 124
Wise, George, 13
Wise, George Spiridion, 13
Wise, Mary, 13
Wise, Mary Sava, 13
Wise, Susan, 108
Wise, Victoria, 13
Wolf, Adeline, 124
Wolf, Anny Elisabeth, 124
Wolf, Henry Drummond, 124
Wolf, Maddalena, 156
Wood, R, 135
Woodehouse, Berkeley, 115
Woodehouse, Laura, 115
Woodford, Alexander, 50
Woodford, Cosmo George Frederick, 50
Woodford, Gordon, 50
Woodford, Lady, 50
Woodhouse, James, 15, 122
Woodley, Emma Louisa, 176
Woodley, John, 127, 191
Woodley, Samuel, 191
Woodley, Sophia, 191
Woodley, Sophia Lissa, 127
Woodley, Thomas John, 127, 130
Woodman, Eliza, 114
Woodman, James, 114
Woodman,, Ellen, 114
Woods, Mary, 69
Woods, Mary Agnes, 69
Woods, William, 69
Woolcombe, -, 206
Worsley, George, 153
Wray, Charles William, 93
Wright, -, 215
Wright, Adam, 84

Wright, Charles, 97
Wright, Edmund Gisbourne Peel, 110
Wright, Henry Press, 110
Wright, James, 215
Wright, John, 164
Wright, Margaret, 164
Wright, Thomas, 173
Wyard, J, 110
Wyatt, J, 155

Y

Yarnley, Annie, 13
Yarnley, Lucy Jane, 13
Yarnley, William Richard, 13
Young, Charles, 139

www.ingramcontent.com/pod-product-compliance
Lightning Source LLC
Chambersburg PA
CBHW022010220426
43663CB00007B/1029